Turn Your Church Inside Out

"Walt Kallestad is an encouraging, inspirational leader. He has committed his life to turning Christian Churches inside out."
  —John C. Maxwell
    Founder, the Injoy Group

"The essence of Walt's personality is found in all his work. He is a leading visionary who can really make things happen. This book shows that pastors everywhere can make great things happen for their congregations."
  —Robert Schuller
    Senior Minister, Crystal Cathedral
    and Hour of Power Ministries

"Walt Kallestad lives what he leads. Now in this book, Walt gives us what he lives: his passion, insight and vision. Any pastor of any sized ministry will find spiritual truth and power for a ministry that really works!"
  —Rev. Michael Foss
    Prince of Peace Lutheran Church
    Burnsville, Minnesota

Also by Walt Kallestad

BUILDING A COMMUNITY FOR OTHERS

TURN YOUR CHURCH INSIDE OUT

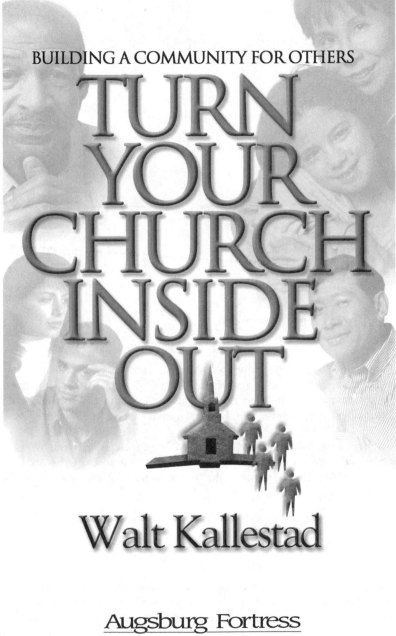

Walt Kallestad

Augsburg Fortress
MINNEAPOLIS

Contents

This book is lovingly dedicated to
all the members and friends of
Community Church of Joy.

You have made the commitments and sacrifices
necessary to turn Community Church of Joy
inside out to build a community for others.

I also dedicate this book to my best friend
and partner in ministry,
my wife, Mary.

Preface

Writing this little book began some twenty-two years ago, when I accepted a call to become pastor of Community Church of Joy in Glendale, Arizona. At the time I could not have imagined the future that is our reality now. As the great Danish theologian, Søren Kierkegaard, wryly put it, life can only be understood backward, but it must be lived forward. Only now can I look back to see with clarity the steps along the way that transformed Community Church of Joy from a struggling *church for ourselves* into a growing, vibrant *community of faith for others.*

This book shares the vision, shares what we have learned about realizing the vision, and offers help along the way for any church that wants to take the transformational journey toward becoming a center for dynamic mission. The book asks and attempts to answer a simple question: What would the church look like if it were truly a church for others? How would worship, preaching, prayer, programming, staffing, financing—all the facets of our common life—have to change for the church to be a radically inclusive community of followers of Jesus?

I invite you to ask the same questions. Read the book. Think and pray about its applicability to your congregation. Let your imagination soar and begin to dream your way into a larger vision for Christian mission. Then share the book with the leadership of your church and engage them in the same imaginative, prayerful venture. Work through the book chapter by chapter; tailor it to your circumstances, and avail yourself of additional tools and resources at www.joyonline.org. And may the Lord bless you on your journey.

This book project would never have been possible without the enormous help and support of my friend Dr. Henry F. French, former vice president at Augsburg Fortress Publishers and presently director of studies with the Division for Global Mission of the Evangelical Lutheran Church in America. He has worked closely and encouragingly with me in the writing and editing of the book. Thanks, Hank!

I also deeply appreciate my daughter, Shawn Marie, for her assistance in transcribing early versions of the manuscript. She was both tireless and uncomplaining.

And how does one thank the people who so faithfully work with you day in and day out in the mission of God? The staff at Community Church of Joy has been through thick and thin in the transformation of our church into a Jesus community for others. We have learned and loved together, and neither Community Church of Joy nor this book would be possible without each and every one of them. Thank you.

A word of sincere thanks also must go to Rev. Marvin Roloff, my dear friend and champion CEO of Augsburg Fortress Publishers. He has a heart for ministry and has supported this project from the beginning.

Finally, I extend a heartfelt thanks to everyone else who has so generously given of their time, talents, and resources to help bring this book to fruition.

Introduction

Under Construction—
A Church for Others

"Joy to the world, the Lord has come."

What you will read in this book is drawn from twenty-two years of experience at Community Church of Joy—twenty-two years of learning how to be a "church for others." Like your church, ours stands as a bearer of a long tradition. We are doing what the church has always done: proclaiming and living the gospel in ways that the people of this time and this place can hear, see, experience, and understand.

For 2,000 years, generation after generation of Christian men and women has built churches that responded to the needs, influences, and dynamics of the cultures they lived in. For 2,000 years, generation after generation of Christians has witnessed to the gospel, the story of God's great love for the world, in ways that were responsive to the social, political, economic, and cultural realities framing their lives. Community Church of Joy tries to continue that witness.

The gospel of God's love and salvation, revealed in Jesus of Nazareth, takes concrete historical expression in the church, the community of those who believe the gospel. This gospel, in the hands of very human—and thus culturally enmeshed, not to mention sinful—people has given rise over the centuries to an incredible variety of institutional forms. From age to age and from place to place, the church has taken on a bewildering diversity of structures, polities, worship styles, devotional habits, forms of leadership, understandings of mission, social agendas, and evangelistic strategies.

If you compare churches from age to age and from place to place, you quickly come to the conclusion that the only thread of continuity between them is the person of Christ and their faith that "in Christ God was reconciling the world to himself" (2 Corinthians 5:19). Down the long centuries, people grasped by this faith have found an amazing number of different forms, structures, rituals, and practices to proclaim it and to live it. Anyone who thinks there is only one way to be church or to do church simply does not understand and appreciate the marvelous symphony and diversity of Christian history. Nor are they likely to understand or appreciate Community Church of Joy.

Too often we have circled our wagons, created little enclaves of piety and worship, built walls around our communities of faith, and invited people in only if they were willing to become like us.

God's people in this time and place continue to live in the real world and continue to be called by God to engage that world in ways that are both faithful to the gospel and responsive to the social and cultural realities of our daily life. Our twenty-first-century world is one of dynamic, continuous, and rapid change. Keeping up is crucial if you want to be relevant in this world. Sadly, many churches have not kept up.

Too often we have circled our wagons, created little enclaves of piety and worship, built walls around our communities of faith, and invited people in only if they were willing to become like us. We have created churches "for us." It is one of the less than positive reactions to cultural change that the church has come up with.

Nevertheless, God is still at work in the world, still loving the world, and still calling people—calling the church—to join in that work and that love. Now, at the beginning of the third Christian millennium, the people of God around the world need to hang a huge sign over the front, back, and side doors of every church for all to see:

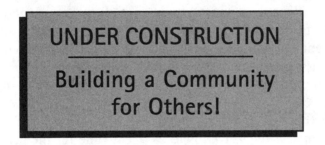

UNDER CONSTRUCTION

Building a Community for Others!

In our increasingly secular, post-Christendom, postmodern world, it is clearly time for the followers of Jesus Christ to deconstruct the church for ourselves in order to begin building churches that genuinely exist for the others in our midst. It is time to start building churches for all those who are either outside or on the margins of faith, as well as for all those who are either on the outside or on the margins of social acceptance.

For far too long the church has existed primarily for those who belong to it. Meeting the spiritual, emotional, and physical needs of church members has been the primary focus of pastors and other church leaders. Don't misunderstand. Meeting the needs of church members is not, in and of itself, wrong. Church members have legitimate needs, and it is legitimate for the church to tend to them. It is illegitimate, however, when caring for church members becomes an end in itself, the primary reason for the church's existence.

I know that I am generalizing and that what I am saying

cannot be said of every church. Nevertheless, generalizations do disclose general truths, and it is not too much to say that the church of our time and our place is largely inwardly focused. It has lost sight of the world outside its walls. Which is to say, the church has also lost sight of the God who works in and loves the world. And that is a genuine tragedy.

God is a missionary God. God moves out in love toward the lost and the aimless, toward those for whom life is empty and meaningless, toward those who are poor, oppressed, and victimized, toward all those who are confused and lonely, and toward those who act out their alienation in addictive or violent behavior. God is a missionary God, and the church must be a missionary church. The church exists for no other reason than to participate in God's mission. *Without mission there is no church.*

It is time for churches everywhere to see things as Jesus of Nazareth saw them. That is to say, it is time for the people of God to become a radically *inclusive* community. Story after story in the written Gospels makes it clear that in Jesus' mind all are invited to sit at God's table. There are no outsiders for Jesus. All are included, all are invited.

Ironically, the only folks in the Gospels who could be called outsiders are those who, out of religious pride and prejudice, *exclude themselves* from God's inclusive reign. In the Gospel stories, it is the religious people who have convinced themselves that *they are the only true insiders* who have unwittingly *cut themselves off* from the all-embracing love of God.

In the ninth chapter of Matthew we find an interesting encounter between Jesus and the religiously correct insiders of his day. It seems they were angry at and critical of Jesus because he ate with tax collectors and sinners. He not only ate with them, he seemed to enjoy and seek out their company.

Now in our ears, the word *sinners* rings with images of immoral or criminal behavior, with images of bad people. Not so in this text. Here in Matthew, *sinners* has the generic meaning of those who, for whatever reasons, fall outside the Jewish law. They are the poor, the lame, the diseased, and those dispossessed of the land, those who may have abandoned faith for one reason or another, all those who either did not or could not go to the synagogue or temple to worship properly. *Sinners* in this generic sense is equivalent to *outsiders*, those who, for whatever reason, were not a part of the believing and worshiping religious community. In conventional religious wisdom they did not belong, and the conventionally religious people were angry at Jesus—an observant Jew—for eating with them.

Jesus' response to their anger was direct and to the point: "Go and learn what this means, 'I desire mercy, not sacrifice [read "religious activities"].' For I have come to call not the righteous [read "insiders"] but sinners [read "outsiders"]" (Matthew 9:13).

Whatever else it might be, the church is not a Jesus community, not truly Christian, if it does not sit down to eat with outsiders. Figuring out just what that means in our world must be at the top of the church's third-millennium agenda.

Archbishop William Temple once exclaimed that the church is the only society in the world that exists for the sake of those who are not members of it. In the same vein, Dietrich Bonhoeffer, writing from a Nazi prison in 1944, stated:

> The church is the church only when it exists for others . . . the church must share in the secular problems of ordinary human life, not dominating, but helping and serving. It must tell people of every calling what it means to live in Christ, to exist for others.[1]

These two visionary theologians saw the church as Christ saw it. Any Jesus community that exists for others and with others is a community after the heart of God. It is a community whose life together is modeled on the life of its founder. At Community Church of Joy, that is what we are committed to be.

It has been a long, hard, but joyful struggle. When I arrived at this church in 1978, it was still very young, having first opened its doors in 1974. A child of its time, Community Church of Joy was showing all the signs of an inwardly focused organization with more ties to the past than to the present and the future.

The ministry to which the congregation had called me was understood as a chaplaincy, as taking care of the spiritual needs of the membership. As the pastor, I was expected to be available to every member whenever and wherever they needed me. I was the minister and they were the subjects of my ministry. Sound familiar? No matter who else was there, if I wasn't at the hospital bedside, in the nursing home, with the grief-stricken, in the counseling room, or any other place they needed me, then the "church" wasn't there. Of such is clergy burnout born!

Those who had called me wanted me to stay close to home. But I thought of the vision that moved Bishop Temple and Dietrich Bonhoeffer. I, too, wanted to build a church for those who didn't go to church, a church for others. I wanted to do away with the insider-outsider mentality, do away with the prerogatives of church membership and affirm the privileges of missionary service in the name of our gracious, loving, and missionary God.

It was not easy. In 1978, about 260 people called themselves members of Community Church of Joy, and on any given Sunday about ninety of them would show up at our small facility for worship. As we enter the new millennium we find ourselves on a 200-acre campus with more than 10,000 people calling themselves members, from 3,000 to 5,000 gathering for celebratory worship each weekend; and over 10,000 gathering for special celebratory services. Tens of thousands of both paid and volunteer hours and millions of dollars in mission-focused resources are spent each year as we respond to the larger community's hunger for God.

We have crafted a welcoming church, a missionary church, a mission center from which—by proclamation and service—the good news of God's love for all people is made concrete, tangible, real. We see as our great privilege the opportunity to bring joy to the heart of God by bringing joy to the world God loves.

Are we the only way to be a church in this postmodern world? Of course not. Are we a creative model for a dynamic and faithful way to be a church that is relevant to the realities of our world? Absolutely. Do we have all the answers? No. Do we have some answers that have stood the test of relevance in this time and place? Yes. And that's what this book is all about—sharing with you some of the things we have learned over the last twenty-two years in our struggle to become and remain a church for others.

The chapters in this little book explore what it means to keep others first in our planning for and practice of ministry. If yours is a large and growing church you will find much here that affirms what you are already doing —and perhaps a few things that will stretch you in new, other-directed ways of ministry.

Are we the only way to be a church in this postmodern world? Of course not. Are we a creative model for a dynamic and faithful way to be a church that is relevant to the realities of our world? Absolutely.

If you are the pastor of a medium-sized church wanting to take the next step, to go to the next level of faithfulness and effectiveness in ministry to and with those others, then you will find here both the encouragement and the practical tools you are looking for.

If you are the leader of a small church with limited resources and perhaps limited vision of the possibilities of growth, then this book is for you as well. Remember, Community Church of Joy started right where you are. We were small, focused on ourselves, limited in resources and vision. All we really had was what you also have—the promise of Jesus to his first little band of followers: "What is impossible for mortals is possible for God" (Luke 18:27).

From small beginnings greatness grows. Any church,

beginning where it is, fueled with a passionate love for the world God loves, can become a harbinger of the reign of God, a place where all are invited, where none are excluded, and where everyone celebrates with joy the presence of God.

Jesus said it well: "The kingdom of heaven is like a mustard seed that someone took and sowed in his field; it is the smallest of all the seeds, but when it has grown it is the greatest of shrubs and becomes a tree, so that the birds of the air come and make nests in its branches" (Matthew 13:31–32).

This book is your invitation to learn from the experience of Community Church of Joy and then—through the interactive wonders of the Internet—to challenge us, to teach us from your own experience, to join us at www.joyonline.org in building a church for a new generation.

1

Celebrating Others

You shall love your neighbor as yourself.
—Leviticus 19:18; Mark 12:31

I literally grew up in the church. My dad was a pastor, and the church was a natural part of my life. From an early age I felt very much at home with both the language and practices of faith.

Church was important to me and I wanted people that were important to me to share it. So I invited my friends to come with me. They usually turned me down. Church, it seems, was not for them.

I went away to college and continued with both weekly worship and Bible study. Again I invited my friends to come. Again they turned me down. Church, it seems, was not for them.

I asked myself why. Why wouldn't these people I cared about, people who were important to me, accept my invitation to go with me to church? It seems there were lots of reasons. They found it boring. They didn't understand the language of worship and faith. The messages they heard seemed, at best, irrelevant to their lives, or, at worst, trite and trivial. They didn't feel genuinely welcomed by the well-dressed folks who obviously belonged. The programs and activities listed in the bulletin didn't seem to be formulated with them in mind.

When they left they didn't feel like coming back because nothing had really touched their souls, nothing had really answered to the longing of their hearts. Church simply wasn't a place for them.

The recurring experience of inviting people I cared about to church and being turned down was the genesis of my call to ministry. I believed (and still do!) in the church as the bearer of good news to a dark and dying world. I believed (and still do!) in the church as the bearer of Christ to a world that desperately needs to meet him, that desperately needs to hear his unconditional invitation to life—abundant, rich, meaningful life today, tomorrow, and forever.

The experience of my friends' turning away from the church gave rise in me to a passionate commitment to become a pastor and build a church where these friends would feel at home, a place they would want to come to because it answered to the needs of their souls, connected them to Christ, and set them free to become followers of Christ. I wanted to build a church for all the others who lived outside the church, either with no faith or on the margins of faith—a place where their presence and their lives would be genuinely celebrated.

We're not building for ourselves

At the opening ceremony for Disney World, Walt Disney, the creative genius behind the theme park, proclaimed, "We didn't build this for ourselves. We built it for others." Disney hit on an excellent motto for the church in our generation. We will not build churches for ourselves. We will build them for others. And we will celebrate their homecomings.

The attitude and behavior of the church must be the same as that of the father in Jesus' well-known parable of the prodigal son. When the son returned from his long sojourn in the world outside his family, his father embraced him, welcomed him, loved him, and threw a party to celebrate his homecoming. The older brother (call him the insider) was angry at the father and wanted nothing to do with the celebration. He was incensed that family resources he thought should be spent on him were spent in celebrating the return of his wayward brother.

And so it is with so much of the church. Insiders all too often want little, if anything, to do with outsiders, and they become angry at the suggestion that outsiders should not only be welcomed but also celebrated. The idea that the church's resources should be liberally spent to make outsiders feel at home does not sit very well with many, if not most, insiders.

Who are the others?

Of course, any talk of building a church for others implies that we know who they are and that we have a theological reason for engaging them. Why should we, who are inside the family of God, care about those who are outside? In what manner, shape, and form should we care about them? To what degree should we care about them? And just who are they anyway? These are good questions worthy of careful consideration by churches eager to be faithful to a missionary God.

To begin with, it is safe to say that the others are not us. They are not churchgoers; they are not people of active Christian faith. This is not a value judgment. It is a simple observation. Some people have Christian faith and some don't. Some people go to Christian churches and others don't. If Bishop Temple, Dietrich Bonhoeffer—and Jesus—are right, then the church exists for them, for their sake and for their salvation. (We'll talk a bit about salvation later. For now, let it be enough to say that salvation means a lot more than just "going to heaven.")

In this time and place, many of the others for whom the church exists know little, if anything, about the church. They know little if anything about Jesus, and nothing about Christian faith. In years past, it was often the case that people who didn't go to church were people who used to go to church. For one reason or another they stopped going. If you spoke with these lapsed Christians about faith, chances were good that they would understand much of the vocabulary. More than likely they would have heard the more familiar Bible stories and would have known some of the more familiar hymns. They may even have attended worship at Christmas and Easter for nostalgia's sake, if for no other reason. In short, there was common ground for conversation about the things of faith.

Not so today. Many of those in a previous generation who left and did not return to the church had children, and those kids grew up with no Christian history and no Christian memory. Jesus is as familiar to them as Krishna, a Hindu deity, is to most Christians. They don't know the difference between the Old and New Testaments, between gospels and epistles, or between any of the many denominations that mark the Christian landscape.

> Tragically, many in our society have tried Christian faith and found it wanting—largely because they have tried the church and found it wanting.

There are millions of people who, having grown up knowing nothing about Christian faith and practice, find themselves dissatisfied with secular materialism, or falling into nihilistic despair, or seeking to still the restlessness of their hearts by wandering among the many New Age, Eastern, or generic spiritualities that commend themselves to today's spiritually hungry.

These others, however, do have a few things in common with us. To begin with, they too were created in the image of God; they too are loved by God; and they too are spiritually restless. To paraphrase St. Augustine—they, like us, will not finally find the rest they seek until they rest in the God who made them and loves them.

Folks with no Christian memory, however, are not the only ones for whom the church exists. There are other others. Tragically, many in our society have tried Christian faith and found it wanting—largely because they have tried the church and found it wanting. If they still have Christian faith at all—and many of them do—they are on its edges or margins, questioning its relevance, doubting much of the church's dogmatic teachings and doctrinaire practices, turned off by the church's exclusiveness, and unconvinced of the church's value in a world where there is no end of organizations and ideologies competing for their attention and loyalty.

It is perhaps harder for those who have tried the church and left to cross that threshold again than it is for those who have never entered a church to do so for the first time. Old, negative experiences die hard. The influence of poor (or perhaps even bad) preaching, teaching, or worship may need to be overcome. Old wounds from little or no hospitality, caring, or compassion may need to be erased by new experiences of warmth and welcome. Histories of conflict may need to be placed in a new context of forgiveness and reconciliation. In short, healing bad memories may need to happen before new experiences can create new realities for people who have been hurt by the church and by those who call themselves Christian.

Tragically, all too many others were once one of us. The fact that they have left the community of faith, however, does not necessarily mean that they are faith-less. All too often it simply means that the church—for whatever reason—let them down. The church, for whatever reason, did not answer to the deep longing of their souls for meaning, peace, joy, spiritual and emotional health, and well-being. The church did not connect them deeply enough to the God from whom these gifts of life come. And it did not connect them deeply enough to Christian people, ordinary men and women who have the same longings as they do but who have discovered how to walk the paths of life with their hands in God's hand.

These others need to be encouraged to return, to come back, to worship once again. The encouragement to do so, however, must be in the form of a promise—a promise that this time it will be different. This time their homecoming will be celebrated.

Including the excluded

We are not quite done identifying the others for whom the church exists. There are still other others. Jesus called them his friends.

Jesus was often criticized for eating with the wrong kinds of people. The socially unacceptable seemed to be quite acceptable to Jesus. He could see the image of God in them, and he himself was an expression of the forgiving love of God for them. He sought them, embraced them, healed and transformed them. A community of those who follow Jesus can do no other. Indeed, no group of Christians can ever be exclusive and still be a true community of Jesus. He leaves no question about it:

> When the Son of Man comes in his glory, and all the angels with him, then he will sit on the throne of his glory. All the nations will be gathered before him, and he will separate people one from another as a shepherd separates the sheep from the goats, and he will put the sheep at his right hand and the goats at the left. Then the king will say to those at his right hand, "Come, you that are blessed by my Father, inherit the kingdom prepared for you from the foundation of the world; for I was hungry and you gave me food, I was thirsty and you gave me something to drink, I was a stranger and you welcomed me, I was naked and you gave me clothing, I was sick and you took care of me, I was in prison and you visited me." Then the righteous will answer him, "Lord, when was it that we saw you hungry and gave you food, or thirsty and gave you something to drink? And when was it that we saw you a stranger and welcomed you, or naked and gave you clothing? And when was it that we saw you sick or in prison and visited you?" And the king

will answer them, "Truly I tell you, just as you did it to one of the least of these who are members of my family, you did it to me." (Matthew 25:31-40)

We serve Christ by taking care of each other. If we are embarrassed by the other, we are embarrassed by Christ. If we despise the other, we despise Christ. If we close the door to the other we close the door on Christ. But, if we truly open ourselves to the other, Christ is in our midst.

In the mystery of faith, Christ comes to us in the other person—particularly in the hungry, the poor and powerless, in those who are sick in body, mind, or spirit, in prisoners, in the unconventional and morally suspect of society, in all those whom polite and conventional society shuns. A hallmark of Jesus' ministry was his frequent table fellowship with the kinds of people who most "good" people wouldn't think of breaking bread with. When the church opens itself to these others, when it seeks them and celebrates them as the brothers and sisters they truly are, then—and only then—is it the kind of community Christ envisioned.

"You told him I was coming!"

Rob and Lisa, lay members of Community Church of Joy, serve those whose only place to sleep is on the streets or in a homeless shelter. It is unsung work. One Sunday they brought a guest to church with them—a young woman (we'll call her Susan). Susan was a prostitute and drug addict whose only address was the streets she walked looking for men who would pay her enough to feed both her frail body and her addiction.

Susan sat with Rob and Lisa toward the back of the worship center looking nervous and no doubt feeling out of place. As the worship began, however, she started to relax; and during the presentation of God's good news of forgiveness and new life in Christ her attention was transfixed on the stage.

When the service was over, Susan turned accusingly to Rob and Lisa and exclaimed, "You told him I was coming!"

"No!" Rob and Lisa responded with genuine surprise. "No, we didn't!"

"Yes, you did. You had to," she insisted. "He was talking to me, right to me all the time!"

On that particular Sunday, Community Church of Joy, a church built for those who don't belong to it, was a place for Susan. Ron and Lisa introduced me to her, and she asked me to pray for her. She wanted me to pray right then, and she wanted my promise that I would keep praying for her. I promised, as did Rob and Lisa. We wrapped that young woman in prayer and in the love of a community of Jesus that really cared about her.

After that Sunday encounter with God through the love of God's people, Susan stayed clean for three days and then voluntarily entered a drug treatment program. She got off the streets and with the help of caring people put her life back together. Some time later, looking at me with a vibrant smile, Susan laughed and said, "You have no idea how it feels to be born again!"

Although she didn't know it that Sunday morning when she first came to Community Church of Joy, *Susan was one of us—* a beloved child of God whose homecoming we were waiting to celebrate. There are other such stories at Joy. Some folks come home to stay. Some stay for a while and then leave. All are celebrated and made to feel welcome and valued.

Celebration—an attitude grounded in God's love for everyone

A church that celebrates others is a church with an attitude. It is an attitude of profound hospitality and an attitude of profound humility. Full of people who have personally experienced the unconditional, radically inclusive love of God, a church that celebrates others welcomes them unconditionally into the widening circle of God's love. We are all, insiders and outsiders alike, hungry people. The only difference between Christians and non-Christians is that Christians know where the feast is, where the party is, and inviting others to the banquet is their special privilege.

To celebrate is a powerful, deeply moving, deeply meaningful reality. As you ponder the various meanings of this word, wonder for a moment what it would be like if *celebration* informed your attitude toward all the others on the other side of the church's door.

The dictionary tells us that to celebrate means to observe an occasion, an event, or a person "with ceremonies of respect, festivity, or rejoicing." To celebrate is to "extol or praise" whatever or whomever it is you're celebrating. It is to "engage in festivities," to throw a party honoring those who are being celebrated.

The thesaurus is full of wonderfully evocative synonyms for celebrate: *make much of, welcome, kill the fatted calf, be hospitable, do honor to, fete, carry shoulder-high, garland, deck with flowers, wreathe, crown, reward, lionize, give a hero's welcome, fling wide the gates, roll out the red carpet, hang out the flags, put out the bunting, blow the trumpets, clash the cymbals, fire a salute, fire a salvo, pay one's respects.*

Take a few moments now and use your imagination. Think about the multitudes of others who live in your community— those on the margins of faith, those without any faith, and those who—for whatever reason—are among the socially excluded. Imagine what your church would be like, what its worship and preaching, programs and services, would be like if these powerful words from the dictionary and thesaurus characterized your congregation's attitudes and behaviors toward them.

Finally it's about serving and loving Christ

The greatest challenge faced by the church in our time is to serve Christ by serving others, to love Christ by loving others. At Community Church of Joy we have, "in fear and trembling," stepped up to this challenge. Our community of faith is centered in Christ, *and therefore* centered in the other. If you don't understand this about us, you won't understand us at all.

We have adopted the attitudes and behaviors of people who genuinely celebrate. We make much of others. We welcome them and kill the fatted calf for them. We are hospitable people. In various and sundry ways we honor the others in our midst. We carry them shoulder-high, garland them, deck them with flowers, wreathe and crown them. We give them a hero's welcome, fling wide the gates, roll out the red carpet, hang out the flags, put out the bunting, blow the trumpets, clash the cymbals, fire a salute—in short, we pay our respects to these beloved children of God.

Do we do it perfectly? No, we don't and we don't expect to. We have simply committed ourselves to try because we believe that it is God's will for the church. We are broken, sinful people, finite people with all the limitations of finitude. But we are God's people, forgiven, strong in our weaknesses because in our weaknesses we rely on Christ.

The starting place is on your knees

Be it figuratively or literally, the true celebration of others begins on your knees in a prayer of confession and repentance. Martin Luther once characterized sin as the state of being curved in on yourself. It is as true of an institution as it is of individuals. You cannot begin to celebrate others until you confess that you are not celebrating others but are celebrating yourself. You cannot be open to others until you confess that you are in practice closed to others and interested only in yourself. You cannot embrace others while you are busy embracing yourself. It simply can't be done.

Confession and repentance make it possible. A church begins the journey toward the celebration of others the moment it confesses how little it truly does celebrate them and repents—not out of guilt or shame, but out of the desire to be people who live Jesus' way. As Rudy Wiebe once wrote:

> Jesus says in his society there is a new way for [people] to live:
>> you show wisdom, by trusting people;
>> you handle leadership, by serving;
>> you handle offenders, by forgiving;
>> you handle money, by sharing;
>> you handle enemies, by loving;
>> and you handle violence, by suffering.
>
> In fact you have a new attitude toward everything, toward everybody. Toward nature, toward the state in which you happen to live, toward women, toward slaves, toward all and every single thing. Because this is a Jesus society and you repent, not by feeling bad, but by thinking differently.[2]

The last phrase is well worth repeating: *"You repent, not by feeling bad, but by thinking differently."* Christians are normally pretty good at taking guilt trips, but wallowing in guilt won't change anything. The Greek word *metanoia*, translated into English as "conversion" or "repentance," literally means a change in one's way of thought, feeling, and behavior. *A repentant person doesn't feel bad—he or she feels good!* With their lives finally in sync with God's love for the world, their lives finally make sense; and that feels very good. As forgiven people, their focus is not on the mistakes, sins, and guilt of the past, rather it is on a present and future of promise and possibility.

A repentant person thinks differently from all those who don't know the ways of God. From all those who find the others of our world inconvenient, or boring and uninteresting, or threatening and frightening, or "different from us," or messy and dirty, or immoral. A repentant person—and a repentant church!—shares God's love for and commitment to the whole human race without distinctions. They think differently because their thinking starts at the cross. Paul knew this well:

> From now on, therefore, we regard no one from a human point of view; even though we once knew Christ from a human point of view, we know him no longer in that way. So if anyone is in Christ, there is a new creation: everything old has passed away; see, everything has become new! All this is from God, who reconciled us to himself through Christ, and has given us the ministry of reconciliation; that is, in Christ God was reconciling the world to himself, not counting their trespasses against them, and entrusting the message of reconciliation to us. (2 Corinthians 5:16-19)

If you "regard no one from a human point of view," if you regard everyone from God's point of view, then you must celebrate them and you must suffer for them, following the example of Christ who suffered out of God's infinite love for us. Nothing else makes sense for a Jesus community.

Thinking differently is not easy— but it is possible

At our church we began the journey toward the others in our community when we began to wonder together what we would be like if we took others as seriously as God did. The thing that makes us most human is the power of our imaginations. When we began to imagine what our church would look like if it was truly a church for others, we began the journey toward celebration. We soon learned that a lot of change was going to be necessary. Change in the ways we worshiped and in the ways we proclaimed the good news. Change in the ways we spent our money, planned our programs, hired our staff, used volunteers, and presented ourselves to the world outside the church.

In the beginning, it was not easy. When I arrived at Community Church of Joy, there was little or no interest in change; and my passionate desire to build a church for others was met with suspicion, distrust, anger, skepticism, and more than a little fear. In talking with countless pastors over the years, I have come to see that the negative response to change that I experienced in those early years was normal and not at all unusual.

My vision for the church seemed dangerous. It threatened to discomfort the comfortable, to remove the squatters, and do away with the entitlement mentality that is the mark of a church turned in on itself. The way I envisioned the church unsettled just about everything and everyone.

My marching orders from the church council were unmistakable: take good care of the membership! I was to visit every member's home at least once a year. I was to make hospital visits daily, counsel regularly, preach weekly, and teach often. It was my job to run the organization, to raise money, chair meetings, and to keep everyone happy as much of the time as possible. Nowhere did my orders from the church council include spending time with "others."

I went to my knees. I prayed for myself and for the church; confessed for myself and for the church; repented for myself and for the church. And then I went out and started meeting, listening to, and learning from others in the neighboring community. I set up luncheons with business leaders, government officials, public school staff members and teachers, social service agents, police, and numerous others. I talked to ordinary folks on the street, in parking lots, shopping malls, and cafés. I asked questions and listened to the answers with as little judgmentalism as I was capable of.

This investment of time, energy, and compassion in others did not endear me to the congregation's insiders. In fact, in the beginning the criticism was ferocious. People were threatened and responded out of their fear. Many left at that time and the irony of it struck deep. We were trying to grow the church and we were getting smaller!

It was a lonely time, but I could not relent. I was—and still am—convinced that God calls the church to share God's commitment of love to the whole of creation. To relent would have meant to surrender my belief that the church exists to serve God's purposes and not its own.

The wondering process

In time, things began to change. Slowly others began to understand my persistence, began to experience God's call, and began to wonder with me what the church would be like if we all took that call seriously. As more and more people began to join in the "wondering process," incremental change became not only possible but inevitable.

Nothing is more powerful in any organization than setting free the imaginations of the people who love the organization and are committed to its health, effectiveness, and faithfulness. This is certainly true of the church. If the imagination pictures a different tomorrow, the will can begin taking steps to realize it today.

Getting people to join the wondering process is not difficult. Just invite them to wonder. It is a very human and very wonder-full thing to do, and you will be surprised at how many people will be eager to join you.

The process begins with an invitation: "Wonder with me for a moment what it would be like if. . . ." For example: "Wonder with me what it would be like if we were really, I mean really, open to others? I wonder what we would do differently, and who would do it. What do you think?"

Make the invitation and then sit back and listen. Listen, question, challenge, guide, and keep the conversation going. Get people in the church wondering together—in meetings and in individual conversations. Keep the conversation going, but keep it real. Real change does not come fast and it does not come easily.

It was during this wondering process that we crafted the mission statement that still directs our ministry today: *That all may know Jesus Christ and become empowered followers, we share his love with joy, inspired by the Holy Spirit.*

The change you are seeking is from self-centeredness to other-centeredness, from celebrating ourselves to celebrating others. Self-centered churches and individuals are self-protective. They avoid risk. They avoid pain. They seek comfort and security. Community Church of Joy was like that back in the late 1970s. We needed to learn that sharing in God's love for the world all too often leads to real suffering with and for those whom God loves. Jesus' life and death bear witness to this truth. It is a truth whose depths we must keep exploring.

Every message, every teaching, every chance conversation is an opportunity to invite people to wonder with you about what God wants and about what the church would be like if it fully committed itself to what God wants. Once the wondering process begins, there is no telling where it will lead. The only certainty is that it will lead to change.

C–E–L–E–B–R–A–T–E
An acrostic to begin with

In the early 1980s, when we had reached a critical mass of people exploring about what it would mean for us to truly become a "church for others," we made nine key decisions to get us started. These commitments were an attempt to put flesh on our decision to celebrate the others in our midst. They were adopted by the leadership of the church and presented to the congregation as behaviors, disciplines if you will, that would begin to turn us into a place where others felt at home.

As an aid to memory and an encouragement to keep them before us, we arranged our nine key decisions into a simple acrostic:

Cheer for others.

Express nonjudgmental love for others.

Listen wholeheartedly to others.

Encourage others.

Build authentic relationships with others.

Receive the gifts of others.

Appreciate others.

Treat others with kindness.

Energize others with grace.

Not very sophisticated, perhaps, but a constant, easily remembered reminder of what we had committed ourselves to.

Cheering for others

One of the first encounters I had as a newly ordained minister was with George. Just before my first congregational meeting began, George walked up to me and informed me that he was going to cast dissenting votes on everything we were planning to propose. I was speechless, and that doesn't happen very often to a preacher! I didn't know how to respond in the face of such negativity.

Without even knowing what we were proposing, or understanding the reasons behind the proposals, George had already made up his mind. He wasn't open to the possibility that change could be good, that he might have something to learn from other people, that new directions might prove to be good directions. He lived in a small world and protected himself from everything outside that world by being negative, by complaining, criticizing, judging, and condemning anything and everyone he didn't know or understand. George was not going to be a cheerleader for the new pastor.

Of course, negative people like George are usually motivated by fear. The unknown is frightening; and for all too many people it seems safer to judge, criticize, and condemn than it does to try to understand.

To *cheer for others* is to stop the cycle of negative thoughts and behaviors that prevent us from really encountering them and getting to know them. To *cheer for others* is to encourage them, to urge them on, to applaud their accomplishments, to salute or acclaim their achievements, to celebrate their contributions. At an even deeper level, cheering for others means risking relationships with them, relationships that just might change the way we think and feel and act because they open us to what the "other" has to give us.

All too often the church's response to everything non-Christian is simple dismissal. Rather than look for the good in our increasingly secular, postmodern culture, we look for the bad, find it, and self-righteously condemn it all.

The church for "others" doesn't do that. A Jesus community that exists for those who don't belong to it is a life-affirming community. It consciously looks for everything in our culture that affirms life, that upholds the dignity of people, and that struggles against evil, violence, and injustice. It deliberately looks for everything in our culture that creates beauty, that exhibits caring and compassion and kindness. And it cheers.

This doesn't mean that the church should be uncritically accepting of everything in our secular, postmodern culture. Any Jesus community worth its name will identify and denounce all within culture that denies life and chooses death. But with equal vehemence it will cheer for anyone and everything that affirms and chooses life—because God chooses life!

Such a church will have a magnetic attraction to others. Rather than feeling judged and dismissed for not being Christian, they will find their own instincts for life affirmed. The cheers of God's people, encouraging them and urging them on, saluting them for their genuine contributions to life, to goodness, justice, and beauty, will be a bridge that crosses the gap between them and the community of faith.

Building a church for others entails changing the very culture of the church. At Community Church of Joy we began appreciating others by first appreciating ourselves. In public venues the positive contributions of individual members to the life of our Jesus community are recognized and celebrated. At every staff meeting applause and cheers are given to folks for a job well done. Examples of jobs well done that are duly noted and saluted range all the way from sparkling bathrooms to great music or drama, from excellent preaching to unheralded missions of mercy, from prayer with a new believer to going the extra mile with a blue-haired, body-pierced teenage skateboarder in the parking lot. Cheerleading makes a difference. Recognizing, encouraging, and applauding the gifts, wisdom, and contributions of members of the congregation becomes the foundation upon which you stand when cheering for others.

Expressing nonjudgmental love

One warm summer afternoon I was standing outside the Bank One baseball stadium listening to my son's band, *Super-Ordinary*, play for the fans before a Diamondbacks baseball game. Suddenly a middle-aged man (call him Doug) left the line heading into the stadium and approached me with a broad smile on his face.

"You had one chance," he said. "One chance."

"What do you mean?" I asked, genuinely puzzled.

"Some time ago," he said, "I was literally ready to kill myself. I was going through a devastating divorce and in so much pain I couldn't stand it."

I could see the pain still etched in his face as he talked about his divorce.

"For some reason," he went on, "the idea of going to church nagged at me. In desperation I thought I would give it a try, but I had made up my mind that if going to church didn't somehow help me I was checking out.

"I got Community Church of Joy's address out of the phone book and went, not really expecting anything good to come of it."

"So what happened?" I asked.

"Well," he said, the smile on his face growing broader. "The completely unexpected. That Sunday in your church I experienced nonjudgmental love. All it would have taken to push me right over the edge would have been judgment and condemnation. Instead I discovered acceptance and love. Now I drive forty-five minutes twice a week with my son to come to church. We don't want to miss anything."

Doug was right. We had one chance, and thank God we didn't miss that chance. It is sobering to wonder how many chances we have missed. Every week there are people like Doug who show up in our churches or at work or who live next door and who are standing on the edge of life's cliff trying to decide what to do. They do not need the moralizing and self-righteousness that is Sunday fare in all too many churches. These cliff dwellers are deeply, infinitely, and unconditionally loved by God. Can the church do any different? Not if it is a Jesus community.

Jesus tells those who follow him, "Be merciful, just as your Father is merciful.

Do not judge, and you will not be judged; do not condemn, and you will not be condemned. Forgive, and you will be forgiven" (Luke 6:36-37).

Try the wondering process on this text. Get members of your congregation to wonder with you what the church would be like (what they would be like!) if this teaching of Jesus were taken with great seriousness—as it should be. I don't think it would be too long before wondering turned into certainty—the certainty that such a church would be a welcoming place, a place of second chances.

I have heard of a seminary professor who, when preaching on the text in Matthew about divorce, told his congregation of seminary students, "Never presume to understand another's pain. Never presume to understand the reasons why people do what they do." It is good advice, and not only for seminary students. We are too ready to judge, too ready to condemn and we drive hurting, confused people away from us. We drive people struggling with the real moral ambiguity of tough choices away from us. We miss our "one chance."

Nonjudgmental love is not a wishy-washy acceptance of anything and everything. True evil must be named and restrained. In a broken, sinful world moral judgments must be made, but they must be made carefully. Nonjudgmental love is open to the experience of others; it wants to understand; it is redemptive love; it wants to heal, not to condemn.

The decision of a community of faith to express nonjudgmental love is the conscious decision to wait for understanding before drawing conclusions about the others in our midst. It is the decision to share the lives of others before judging those lives. All of which leads us to the third key decision underlying our initial commitment to celebrate others.

Listening wholeheartedly to others

I ride a Harley Davidson motorcycle. It is a beautiful machine, and one of my great passions is to roar down a lonely road under a blue sky in the hot desert sun, surrounded by rugged mountains and engulfed in the rich browns and greens of sand and cactus. It's exhilarating. And riding with other Harley aficionados is even greater because a joy shared is a greater joy.

Not too long ago, I rode my Harley to a nearby strip mall on a shopping errand. I hopped off in front of the local Starbucks and decided to go in for a cup of coffee. I noticed several other Harleys parked in front of the coffee shop. Inside, several rough motorcycle riders were crowding the tables, talking and laughing loudly while drinking their coffee. One of them had noticed me getting off my motorcycle, and the fraternal feelings of Harley lovers overcame the suspicion and derision he must have felt for me as a middle-aged and well-dressed man.

"Hey, Harley-man," he called out as I entered the shop. "Come on over and talk dirty with us."

I said I would as soon as I got my coffee, and I did. And they were talking dirty! They made a place for me at the table and for a few moments the conversation was mostly about Harleys. They asked about my bike: how long had I had it, where did I ride, was I a member of a club? Then a brief lull in the conversation was broken when one of them asked me, "So, what do you do?"

"I'm a Christian minister," I said, and you could have heard a pin drop. A wonderful mix of confusion—what was I doing talking with them!—and discomfort—what were they doing talking to me!—passed over their faces.

"So, any of you guys go to church?"

A chorus of half-defiant, half-embarrassed replies of "no" answered my question.

"Ever think about God?"

"Well, yeah."

"I don't know, well, sometimes, I guess."

"Well, you know, not a lot. Like, you know, now and then."

"Well, then," I asked, genuinely curious, "why don't you go to church?" With that, I shut up and listened.

And they talked. I heard a lot of things that helped me understand both the world they lived in and the impassable barriers they believed existed between their world and the world of those who went to church. Finally it was fear that kept them away, the fear of exclusion, the fear of being judged and found wanting, the fear of being different and not understood, the fear of not understanding what was going on, the fear of not knowing what to do and how to do it should they ever dare to cross the threshold between their everyday world and the church.

Then it was my turn to talk—a turn I had earned by listening to them. I had listened with no moralizing, no judging, and no quick advice. I had listened only because I wanted to know and understand them, and I wanted to hear what they had to say about the church I loved. They seemed to understand my motives, and so they too were willing to listen.

The church's calling is simply to welcome people as they are into a new and continuing encounter with God.

All I did was offer them an invitation and the promise of welcome. I told them that Community Church of Joy was a place for them and that if they would come perhaps they could meet in a new way the God they sometimes thought about on the back of their Harleys or late at night when there is no one to talk to but themselves.

Will they come? I don't know. They said they would think about it and they seemed serious. Whether they come or not, however, at least they have had the experience of being listened to, of speaking with *a Christian who found them interesting!* They will think about that, and perhaps they will give the church another chance.

The church's job is not to change people arbitrarily to fit some preconceived notion of what a Christian looks like. It is not our job to get folks to conform to some normative pattern of "Christian" living. In fact, I don't believe there is such a thing. There are as many different ways of being Christian as there are people who follow Christ. We are all wonderfully different and unique, and we need the freedom to express our faith in ways that are unique to who we really are. If there is anything normative about being Christian, it is the love that draws us to God, binds us to Christ, and flows through us to others.

The church's calling is simply to welcome people *as they are* into a new and continuing encounter with God. This is not relativism. It is not saying that anything and everything is OK. It is saying, however, that life-changing grace comes only from the transforming power of God. It is grace that brings people to the community of faith and grace that brings about transformation.

Learning to listen, then, is a Christian spiritual discipline. We are usually far too eager to speak, to rebuke, to correct, to guide, to give advice than we are simply to listen to, understand, and share another's experience. Those who speak without listening usually have an agenda they want to impose on others. They want to change others to be more like themselves. Those who really listen, however, are open to the experience of others and are willing to be changed themselves. A listening church, a church that truly celebrates others is a dynamic, changing church because it is constantly enriched by the wealth of experience that others bring into it. To listen to another person with the interest and carefulness that says, "I have nothing else to do and nowhere I'd rather be than with you" is characteristic of Christians who have learned the joy of celebrating others.

Encouraging others

As you practice careful listening you will hear story after story of failing courage. Stories from folks who are ready to give up, discouraged by failure, by broken relationships, by dashed dreams, by lost opportunities. Stories from folks who are frightened, fearful of overwhelming responsibilities, of financial insecurity, of the fast pace and challenge of continuous change, of the indiscriminate violence of modern life. Stories of people who are just plain tired out, fatigued by too much work, by family schedules and responsibilities, by all the claims of all the people and organizations that want their time, their energy, and their money. Stories of people who are sick and tired of being sick and tired, worn down by lack of exercise, by addictive behaviors, by having no seasons of rest and rhythms of relaxation in their lives.

We hear these stories not only from those outside the church but also from those inside the church. Non-Christian or Christian, it takes courage to live in American society. It takes courage to craft lives that have meaning, purpose, and balance. It takes courage to keep doing what needs to be done to care for those who depend on you. It takes courage to explore healthy change, to carve out of the chaos of modern life a way of life that makes sense to you, that answers to your passions, uses your gifts, is self-respectful and respectful of those around you. It takes courage to live, and yet so many in our society seem to be discouraged, disheartened, on the edge of giving up.

The more we hear such stories of discouragement, the more we have committed ourselves as a Jesus community to the spiritual discipline of encouragement. We deliberately work to create a culture where genuine encouragement of one another is just as natural as greeting one another when we meet. It spills over. As encouragement becomes part of the air we breathe inside the church, it becomes a natural response to the discouragement we daily meet outside the church.

It is true that only those with courage can encourage. If we want to be a church that truly celebrates others, then we must be people of courage ourselves; and we can only get that courage from God and from each other. Encouraged within the community of faith, we become wellsprings of courage for the men, women, and children who populate our lives outside the community of faith.

Building authentic relationships

The church is about nothing at all if it is not about relationships—our relationship with God and our relationships with each other. Love, justice, compassion, caring, kindness, sacrifice, service—these are not nice ideas to be thought about in the safety of solitude. They are the very substance of life lived out in the risky, messy, glorious gift of relationships.

Todd Hahn, a Christian leader committed to understanding

and working with young people who inhabit a postmodern world, has insightfully noted that, "Postmodern people crave relationships and will gravitate to places and people where authentic relationships are being created."[3]

The key word is *authentic*. An authentic relationship is one that does not have an ulterior motive. It is not a means to an end, it is an end in itself. As Hahn noted, young people—perhaps all people—in our postmodern world are *tired of being used* and are naturally suspicious of all relationships that seem to have hidden agendas.

We want to be wanted for who we are and not just for what we do or give or bring. Few things drive others away from the church more quickly than the feeling that they are valued only as a statistic on a new member report, or as a new giving unit, or as fodder for the insatiable hunger for more and more volunteers in the various programs of the church.

People are increasingly weary of feeling that their value lies only in their usefulness, in their productivity, in their ability to create wealth, accomplish tasks, and give pleasure. Perhaps that is why Eastern spiritualities with their emphasis on *being* rather than *doing* are so attractive to so many Americans. Perhaps that is why we need to refocus on those Christian spiritual disciplines that foster intimacy with God as the ground of our intimacy with each other. After all, in the divine relationship there are no conditions, only acceptance.

If Todd Hahn is correct, and I suspect that he is, when the church becomes a place where relationships have more than instrumental value, it will be a place that people seek rather than flee. At Community Church of Joy we have been delighted to discover that the simple acrostic we came up with to keep before us our decision to C-E-L-E-B-R-A-T-E others has slowly but surely moved us toward authenticity in our relationships both inside and outside the church. As we practiced the spiritual disciplines of cheering, nonjudging, listening, and encouraging, we began to experience the wonder, variety, and value of other people in new and enriching ways. We discovered that just knowing them is a surprising gift. We have also discovered that we—just as we are—are also surprising gifts for them.

Receiving the gifts of others

One of the most difficult things many of us face is admitting that "others" may know more than we do, may have better ideas and clearer vision than we do, may be more skillful than we are, and perhaps may even be more passionate and eager than we who have been carrying the burden for so long. Enthusiastic others can be annoying!

It is natural to want others to quietly fit in, to respect the way things have always been, and not upset our usual arrangements. It is also the natural way to a stagnant and dying church, one that others will stay away from.

When people from outside come inside, they bring with them a rich infusion of fresh blood, new insights and perspectives, an expanded vision, and the skills to make things happen in perhaps new and challenging ways. It can be upsetting. It can also be exhilarating!

This is axiomatic: *To be a church for others is to be a church that embraces change.* You can't bring a whole lot of new people into an organization and not expect creative challenges to the status quo. You can't increase the talent pool and not expect new things to happen. You can't increase the number of people with their own unique sets of needs and not expect new needs to surface. A church that embraces others must embrace change. Not begrudgingly but gratefully.

Change is embraced to the degree that you receive the gifts that others bring with genuine gratitude and with a willingness to facilitate their use creatively. It will not always be easy, and there are will always be some who will resist change. Nevertheless, embracing the gifts of knowledge and talent, of insight and ability that others bring will strengthen and invigorate any community of faith beyond its capacity to imagine.

Receiving the gifts of others also has to do with openness

to the knowledge, skills, and technologies of so-called secular culture that can help the church be more efficient and effective in stewarding its resources, proclaiming its gospel message, teaching its values, and meeting the real needs of real people. A church that denies the positive values and technologies of secular culture lives in an unreal world and cannot expect to be taken seriously by those whose lives are lived outside its closed doors.

One final word about receiving the gifts of others. When we think about gifts, our minds naturally gravitate to thoughts about the "gifted." We think about successful and competent people who seem to cope well with the modern world. We think about educated, knowledgeable, skillful folks—folks not unlike ourselves. It is good to receive the gifts of these others, but we should never forget that there are "other others" who also have gifts to give.

Men and women who work with the poor, the homeless, the unemployed and uninsured, with those who have succumbed to self-destructive, addictive behaviors, with the physically and mentally disabled, with the elderly and infirm, have discovered that such folks also have things to teach us and gifts to give us. Such folks often have deeper insights into their own lives and into the social and relational conditions that provide the context for their lives than do the people who try to help them. They have stories to tell, and those stories are a gift to us who believe in the gospel of the cross. We meet God in their stories. At Community Church of Joy we have learned—and are still learning—how to receive and grow from these gifts as well.

Appreciating others

The highest form of appreciation is respect. Let me tell you the story of Erin Gurell, a young teacher in the inner city of Long Beach, California, who knew the meaning of appreciation and dared to respect at-risk kids who, in their young lives, had experienced little more than contempt from most adults. Erin could see that her students were without hope and dreams. Many were experimenting with drugs. Others were constantly in and out of jail. Some were living in the streets without family support.

Other teachers had used the old ways to reach these kids but had failed miserably and given up. These kids were certainly not appreciated—until, that is, Erin became their teacher. She stacked the old textbooks in the corner and brought in new books and music and materials that taught the basics by using real-life, interactive examples the kids could relate to.

This cost money and there was no budget for it; so Erin got extra jobs to pay for her new creative materials and methods out of her own pocket. She took her students on field trips, also at her expense. She kept her classroom open until midnight, tirelessly working with her students, helping them to write their own stories, which were eventually bound into a book called *Freedom Writers*.

It was a life-changing experience for those kids—all because a young woman appreciated the mystery and wonder of their young lives and wouldn't give up on them. Instead, she stepped outside the box and those kids were, in their own words, "born again."

Because Christians believe in "God the Father Almighty, Creator of heaven and earth," we should respect and appreciate all life; we should revere all life; we should stand in awe before the mystery of life. Respect has to do with recognizing value. Foundationally, Christians appreciate and respect others because God values them. Every life—even those that from our limited perspective may seem frivolous or wasted or useless or even evil—is hidden in the silence of God and wrapped in the mystery of God's love.

Jesus was respectful to prostitutes, tax collectors, thieves, murderers, drunkards, poor people, and others considered outcasts of society. Never once did Jesus condemn them. He loved them, forgave them, called them, offered them new choices and new possibilities. Those that he censured were the disrespectful, the judgmental, the indifferent and unloving.

The church that has decided to celebrate others must genuinely respect all races, all classes, and all ages. It is a church that celebrates diversity and stands in awe before the mystery of God's creative love expressed in every person. It is a church that welcomes the divorced, single parents, the mentally ill, and people with disabilities. It is a church whose celebration translates into loving kindness.

Treating others with kindness

The best short description of the Christian lifestyle comes out of the Old Testament. The prophet Micah lets us know exactly what God wants from God's people: "He has told you, O mortal, what is good; and what does the Lord require of you but to do justice, and to love kindness, and to walk humbly with your God?" (Micah 6:8). Now there's a good text for the wondering process.

Wonder with me for a moment. What would we be like if we really did justice? If we really loved kindness? If we really walked humbly with our God? I think we would be different. A true Jesus community must wonder about such things and, having wondered, must try to live as it imagines God would have it live.

Recently I visited a homeless shelter. On a tattered sign on a tattered wall, I read: "Please be kind." Words of desperation by men and women who have not experienced the world as a friendly or generous or caring and compassionate place. You shouldn't have to ask for kindness—especially within and from a Jesus community.

A church for others will value such things: friendliness, generosity, caring and compassion, gentleness, considerateness, forbearance, tolerance. Such things create an atmosphere that is wonderful to breathe. Such things beget themselves.

We have large parking lots at Community Church of Joy. They are irresistibly tempting to the "skater rats," mostly young boys, often with blue, red, or green hair, oversized clothes, tattoos, and body piercing. After seeing them riding their skateboards back and forth in the parking lot, some handymen in the church got together and built ramps for the skaters to jump and do tricks on. It was a simple kindness. On occasion we go out in the parking lot and serve them pizza. It too is a simple kindness. There are no strings attached. We are just letting them know that they are appreciated. I suspect that doesn't happen to them very often.

It gets hot in the summer in Phoenix, sometimes brutally so. It is not uncommon at such times for young people in the church to go to the parks and hand out free bottles of water to any who thirst for a cold drink. It is a simple kindness. Again, no strings attached.

There is a theological mystery here, the mystery of Christ present in human need. The leaders of our youth help them to hear the voice of Christ, "I was thirsty and you gave me a drink." Strange how the simple giving of a bottle of cold water to a thirsty person can become a sacrament of the presence of Christ for those who follow Christ.

Kindness comes as such a surprise in our indifferent, impersonal world. A gratuitous generosity of spirit is striking in an increasingly mean-spirited society. People are so angry today. Rage seems to lie just below the surface everywhere, ready to erupt at the least provocation. In a mean-spirited world, kindness is shockingly unexpected and yet hungered for.

It is not without reason that Paul lists kindness as one of the nine fruits of the Spirit in Galatians 5:22. Kindness is one of the distinguishing marks of a true Jesus community for the kindness of God's people is a mirror of "the immeasurable riches of his grace in kindness toward us" (Ephesians 2:7). Any church that has made the decision to be a "church for others" has at the same time chosen the way of justice, kindness, and a humble walk with God.

Energizing others with grace

"For by *grace* you have been saved through faith, and this is not your own doing; it is the gift of God . . ." (Ephesians 2:8). The Gospel is about grace or it is about nothing. It is about grace or it is not "good news." It so easy to lose sight of this foundational truth. We can become so busy with the business of God that we forget that "it is God who is at work in [us], enabling [us] both to will and to work . . ." (Philippians 2:13). We can become so preoccupied with celebrating others that we lose sight of the fact that God delights in us and in our own homecoming. We can be so distracted by our commitments that we forget that we ourselves have been and are being celebrated.

Worship is participation in God's celebration of us. Through the words that we speak, the music that we sing, the water of baptism, and the bread and wine of Jesus' meal we bathe ourselves in grace. We remind ourselves over and over again of the unlimited, unconditional, unsparing mercy and compassion of God. We bring ourselves into the presence of God knowing that God is present to meet us. We bring our weariness, our confusion and doubts, our resistance, our diseases, our brokenness, and our sin. We bring our dreams and hopes and expectations, our needs and desires, our passions and ambitions. We bring our anger and our joy, our sorrows and our happiness, our fear and our courage, our unwillingness and our willingness. In short, we bring our humanity, we bring all of ourselves into the presence of God as honestly as we can, trusting grace, trusting that we will be loved, forgiven, and strengthened for the journey.

God's celebration of us is our celebration of grace. In that grace is the faith, courage, wisdom, and strength to go out into the world and invite others to come and join the celebration of their own homecoming. Grace energizes for no other reason than that grace is the gift of life. When God's people celebrate with abandon the grace they have received and experienced, the gift of life is offered to all and any who enter the circle of their celebration. That's what worship is all about—living in the energies of grace.

As we are with ourselves, we are with others.

As we lived with our acrostic:

Cheer for others.

Express nonjudgmental love for others.

Listen wholeheartedly to others.

Encourage others.

Build authentic relationships with others.

Receive the gifts of others.

Appreciate others.

Treat others with kindness.

Energize others with grace.

we began to discover that the nine key decisions we had made to support our decision to become a "church for others" were spiritual disciplines. And as we began to practice these spiritual disciplines, we began to discover that the attitudes we wanted to have toward others were the attitudes we needed to have toward ourselves.

The decision to celebrate others made no sense at all unless we were simultaneously celebrating ourselves. So we cheer for each other. We try not to judge each other. We listen to each other and encourage each other. We work at building authentic relationships, and we seek to be open to the gifts everyone brings. We are appreciative of one another, and we value kindness as chief among the fruits of the Spirit. Finally, we come again and again, as children of God, to the wellsprings of grace. We drink deeply and then go about our business in the world of others as grace-full people.

I don't want to sound holier than thou. At Community

Church of Joy we are not plaster saints. We are human; we make mistakes and we sin. But we believe with Paul that God's grace is sufficient for us and that the power of Christ is made perfect in our weakness, in our humanness. For that reason alone, we really believe that we can make a difference.

In this chapter I have endeavored to point out the attitudinal and behavioral changes that we worked at early on in order to begin moving toward the goal of building a church for others. It has not been easy, and we are still learning the depths of how to practice these foundational spiritual disciplines of a church that exists for those who don't belong to it.

One thing is clear—it all begins with a decision. Any who choose—as an act of faith and will—to become a church for others, and then choose to practice the spiritual disciplines enumerated in our simple acrostic—C-E-L-E-B-R-A-T-E—will have started on an amazing journey. What begins as an exercise of the will becomes a matter of the spirit. In time the disciplines are transformed from things you do into who you are. It is an amazing and delightful transformation.

Our journey began with the decision to become a church for others and the decision to change our attitudes and behaviors toward others. In the chapters that follow, I will share how these new attitudes and behaviors were reflected in everything we do, in the structures, policies, and programs of the church.

Questions to ponder, things to do

• Has your church made a conscious decision to become a "church for others"? If not, what needs to be done to prepare people for such a decision?

• Of the three kinds of others mentioned in this chapter:
  – People who once attended church but who have stopped coming
  – People with no Christian history or memory

— Those whom conventional society excludes and
discriminates against

Which others would your congregation be most comfortable
with? What needs to be done to move your congregation outside their comfort zone?

• Does your congregation truly *celebrate* others? If yes,
what are the signs of celebration? If no, what are the signs
that celebration is not happening?

• Plan a worship service of confession and repentance that
communicates a new level of commitment to reach the others
in your community through proclamation and service with the
good news of Jesus.

• Review the CELEBRATE acrostic. Which of these spiritual
disciplines of a church for others are currently practiced in
your community of faith? What would you need to do to
implement or increase the practice of these disciplines among
your members?

• Develop a strategy for using the "wondering process" (see
page 30) as a planning tool in helping your congregation
become a community for others.

But we had to celebrate and rejoice,
because this brother of yours was dead and has
come to life; he was lost and has been found.

—Luke 15:32

2

Praying for Others

*Whatever you ask for in prayer with faith,
you will receive.*

—Matthew 21:22

One evening as the sun was setting with its usual dazzling display of grandeur, I followed a dirt road that cut through a 200-acre orchard that I, along with some of Joy's leaders, had been praying about. We were wondering if we should try to purchase it. These 200 acres of orange trees seemed like the perfect place to relocate our growing congregation. The property had great appeal to many of our members and friends, but the best we could offer—since we had no money—was our prayers.

At the end of the winding dirt road was a run-down trailer home. It looked like it was inhabited. There was a car under a leaning tin shed and a rusty mailbox was stuck out by the road inscribed with the name "Scotty."

I knocked on the door, and after a moment it opened. An elderly man dressed in farmers' bib overalls stood in the doorway. I introduced myself and explained that I was the pastor of Community Church of Joy. I explained that many at the church were praying about this orchard, wondering if God would provide a way for us to buy it and build a new

51

center for mission with a worship center, a Christian school, a seniors' center, a place for youth, and much more.

The old gentleman grabbed my arm and pulled me in. He told me his name was Scotty and asked me to follow him to the kitchen table where his wife, Ruthie, was sitting. As I entered the kitchen Scotty said, "Reverend, please tell my wife what you just told me."

So I told Ruthie about our dream of purchasing the land in order to build a new center for ministry. Ruthie started to cry. I noticed Scotty was crying too, large tears running down his grizzled face.

Trying to regain his composure, Scotty eagerly said, "Reverend, my wife Ruthie and I moved to this land forty years ago. Five acres of these orchards belong to us. Nearly every day for the last forty years we walked around our orchard holding hands and praying that one day there would be a great church built here."

I lost my composure and joined my tears to theirs. It was one of those holy moments when you sense the mysterious moving of God's spirit. When I was still a very young child, this couple was praying passionately for something that I was to become a part of forty years later. And now our church was about to become God's answer to their prayer. It staggers the imagination. My heart exploded with joy, and I was more convinced than ever that God was doing something much bigger than I was dreaming of.

We pay a lot of lip service to prayer and we pray a lot, but how many truly believe that it matters, that it makes a difference?

Eventually Community Church of Joy was able to purchase the entire orchard along with the five acres of land that Scotty and Ruthie owned. Ruthie died before the construction began; but she died knowing that it would begin, knowing that God had answered her prayer.

And now for the rest of the story. To this day Scotty, who turned ninety years old on August 1, 1999, still prays for his old property. If you look across our campus to the far edge of the property, you will still see Scotty's old trailer. He asked if he could stay there in exchange for promising to continue to pray for the church he had started praying for almost fifty years ago. We gladly agreed to Scotty's request, and so he stayed on the land and walked the land and prayed for the church we are building until only recently, when deteriorating health necessitated his move to a local nursing home.

Every morning, before the sun got too hot or in the evening when things started to cool off, you could see Scotty walking alone around the campus, his old body stooped over, his hands folded in front of him, his lips moving. As Scotty walked the land each day, praying for the ministries and people of Community Church of Joy, he was faithfully obeying God's will that we pray for the others in our midst. Scotty is for us an icon of God's great love for the world.

"It is faith to see God at work in the world. . . ."

People like Scotty humble us. He is a simple man with a simple faith—but with his simple faith he reaches to profound depths of grace that many of us do not reach. His solitary, praying figure has been a sacrament for us of God's presence. He has focused our attention on the fact that God is indeed present and active in our midst. He has reminded us of Paul's admonition: "Do not worry about anything, but in everything by prayer and supplication with thanksgiving let your requests be made known to God. And the peace of God, which surpasses all understanding, will guard your hearts and your minds in Christ Jesus" (Philippians 4:6-7).

It is time to wonder again, time to wonder what would we be like if we didn't worry? What would we be like, how would we be different if, "by prayer and supplication with thanksgiving," we simply made our requests known to God and then *went on about our business*—our mission—with confidence, trusting that God was present, listening and active among us? I suspect that this would be a tremendous leap of faith for all too many congregations and Christians. We pay a lot of lip service to prayer and we pray a lot, but how many truly believe that it matters, that it makes a difference, that prayer is more than well-meaning but ultimately empty words?

In the eighteenth century a form of Christian religion known as deism spread throughout the American colonies. It had a profound influence on the founders of our nation and the framers of the U.S. Constitution. The God of deism has been compared to a watchmaker who creates an intricate timepiece, winds it up, sets it running, and then leaves it and goes off, perhaps to make another. Deism was a way to believe in the existence of a creator God without having to involve that God in the day-to-day running of the universe. It was a way to emphasize both human moral responsibility and the natural working of the natural laws of a mechanistic universe. There is certainly little room for mystery or miracle here.

Deism, it seems to me, is alive and well in our time. And it still allows us to have our cake and eat it too—to believe in God and not have to worry about what God may or may not be doing in the world. Christians quite naturally believe in God. Christians believe that God created the world and that "in Christ God was reconciling the world to himself." But for all too many Christians it is just history. Creation and redemption are *what God did in the distant past,* and we act as if we believed that, having done it, God has gone off somewhere else in the universe to do something more interesting, leaving us to get on with the business of the kingdom. It is a very heroic view of the church and its grave responsibility, but it cuts the church off from its greatest resource—the active presence of God!

I get around a lot and hear a lot of sermons in lots of different churches. Most of them are little more than history lessons. They tell you *what God did,* and they tell you what we ought to be doing as a result of what God has done. But they don't tell you *what God is doing*. At Community Church of Joy, what God is doing right now is what we are most interested in.

Walter Rauschenbusch, a theologian of the Social Gospel Movement at the turn of the twentieth century, wrote with penetrating insight that, "It is faith to see God at work in the world and to claim a share in his job."[1] Faith does not focus only on what God has done in the past; it is vitally interested in what God is doing among us right now, in this time and in this place. Faith wants to be active in whatever God is doing; for in claiming its share in God's present and ongoing mission, faith is transformed into faithfulness.

God is busy inviting all people into the fullness of life, into the fullness of *shalom*, the all inclusive well-being that has been God's intention for all in creation. Jesus said it clearly, "I came that they may have life, and have it abundantly" (John 10:10). And then he said to his followers, "Peace be with you. As the Father has sent me, so I send you" (John 20:21). Those who follow Jesus, who do mission in the way of Jesus, are sent as Jesus was sent—so that others may have life and have it abundantly.

In the midst of a society that chooses death, a society whose habits and addictions, whose values and vagaries, whose greed and pettiness, whose violence and vindictiveness, lusts and obsessions, spread darkness across the landscape, Christians are called to be light and to witness through what they say and how they live to the abundant life that is in Christ. If we are truly sent as Jesus was sent, then we are visible signs of God present in the world and we have no option but to be a church for others.

The conclusion is obvious: we must live that divine presence first through prayer. If God is truly present and active, and not off somewhere else leaving us bereft of divine guidance and power, then prayer—the two-way communication between the human and the divine—becomes the number one priority and principle activity of those who answer the call to follow Christ. Both for the community of faith as a whole and for individual members of a Jesus community, nothing is more important than prayer.

Changing directions through prayer and the word

When I became the pastor of Community Church of Joy, prayer was not at the center of mission for either me or the congregation. Certainly we prayed. Prayer was a part of worship. We prayed before meetings. I prayed for the sick and the suffering in hospitals or homes. I prayed at weddings and funerals, and always said grace before the ubiquitous church potluck dinner. Yet, for me, and I suspect for most of our people, prayer was more a matter of rote, ritual, and routine than a deep, energizing conversation with the God who loves, calls, sends, and goes with us in mission.

After many months of ministry at this church, I started to feel very empty and uneasy. I didn't know why, but I had this gnawing, churning feeling that something needed to change. I was spiritually dry. Prayer seemed an exercise in futility. I went through the motions of ministry but there was no life to it, no enthusiasm, no vision and excitement. Something had to change. I didn't know what, but I knew that whatever it was it had to change in me if I was to be a catalyst of change for the congregation.

During those early days of my ministry at Joy, I gradually discovered what spiritual teachers have taught for millennia: a spiritual life without discipline is impossible. That was my problem. My lack of spiritual discipline was reflected in the congregation. It is an elemental fact of leadership that as the leader goes, so goes the group. I couldn't model spiritual discipline because I didn't have any.

It was a conference I attended at Stanford University that started me on the road to discipline. I like to believe it was more than coincidence and that God was connecting my need with those who could guide me. Among the many excellent speakers, one in particular really connected with my need. Dr. David Hubbard spoke with a conviction drawn from the crucible of personal experience on the dynamics of prayer and the place of prayer in effective, faithful Christian life and ministry. I soaked it up like a sponge. As I listened, unbidden tears started flowing down my face. At first I was embarrassed. Then I laughed. I realized that the Holy Spirit was moving within me, inviting me to risk personal growth through disciplined daily devotions and prayer.

God wasn't condemning me for not having been more deliberate and disciplined in my personal prayer and devotional life. God simply took me where I was and invited me to begin there. It was an experience of promise rather than judgment, an experience of grace.

I left Stanford and returned to Community Church of Joy with new vigor, vitality, and determination flowing through my spiritual veins, cells, and fibers. I had discovered the obvious—the beginning of discipline is the decision to be disciplined.

Daily prayer times became a regular part of my mornings, taking priority over the business and busyness that clamored for my attention. Eventually prayer spilled out of those disciplined times set aside for prayer and became an ongoing, fairly continuous awareness of God's presence in all that I did, wherever I went. I begin to understand what Paul meant when he admonished the Christians under his care to "Rejoice always, *pray without ceasing*, give thanks in all circumstances; for this is the will of God in Christ Jesus for you" (1 Thessalonians 5:16-18). That had never made sense before. Once the discipline of prayer was transformed into a life of prayer, all of life is thanksgiving.

I disciplined not only my prayer life. I also started on a plan to read through the Bible during the next year. There is a wonderful synergy between prayer and the Bible. Reading daily through the Scriptures provided focus, instruction, insight, and guidance for my prayer. Studying the prayers and the experiences of the ancient people of God provided fresh encouragement for me.

I know I am saying the obvious, but sometimes it needs to be said. When I look at my own life and reflect on con-versations I have had with hundreds of pastors over the years, it becomes tragically clear how often in the busyness of ministry the ground of ministry—prayer and the Word—are neglected.

Along the way, I felt a gentle transformation taking place. The desire to build a church for others that had first driven me into ministry was transformed into the desire to pray for them. Building such a church became an answer to prayer rather than the goal of my ministry. The goal of my ministry became simply to share in and express the love that God has for "the world" (John 3:16).

This deeper understanding of the will and ways of God begins to move the community toward those others who live outside the circle of God's blessing.

Things started changing at Community Church of Joy. With all the enthusiasm of a new convert, I talked with any and all who would listen about what I was experiencing in the daily disciplines of prayer and Bible reading. I developed a message series on prayer and taught the devotional reading of the Bible. I challenged the people of Joy to find out for themselves what I was talking about, and many of them took up the challenge.

It was amazing. We learned together that prayer is indeed two-way communication. For most of us, prayer had been a monologue, a dreary recitation of personal needs and desires. When we took a close look at the content of our prayers, at *what* we prayed about, it was embarrassing. Our prayers amounted to little more than a laundry list of personal wants presented to God as some kind of a cosmic butler whose only business was to do our bidding. Of course, God didn't do our bidding.

In the "school of prayer," built on the foundation of Bible reading, we began to "hear" God. We began to learn of God and to know God in deeper, richer ways than before. We began to understand that prayer was not the delivery of a laundry list of needs, it was a dynamic, two-way conversation in which we both heard and accepted the invitation to join in God's mission. As more and more of us experienced a more profound awareness of God's presence through disciplined lives of prayer and Bible reading, our internally focused ministry began to change. We began to understand that we were chosen to be Christian for a purpose and that God's purpose was far greater than our own salvation.

In fact, 1 Peter 2:9 goes straight to the point: "But you are a chosen race, a royal priesthood, a holy nation, God's own people, *in order that* you may proclaim the mighty acts of him who called you out of darkness into his marvelous light." God has always chosen and sent people to proclaim and make real God's blessing, God's salvation.

The first recorded instance of this was in the very creation of God's people when God called Abraham and Sarah and told them to leave their homeland and go to a land that God would show them. God said to them, "I will make of you a great nation, and I will bless you, and make your name great, *so that* you will be a blessing. . . . And in you all the families of the earth shall be blessed" (Genesis 12:2-3). God's purpose is clear: the choosing and sending of some people for the blessing of all people. Through disciplined prayer and Bible study a richer understanding of God and God's purposes becomes possible for any community of faith that seeks God's will. This deeper understanding of the will and ways of God begins to move the community toward those others who live outside the circle of God's blessing.

"Lord teach us to pray. . . ." (Luke 11:1)

As the interest in prayer begins to spread, people begin asking those in leadership positions to teach them how to pray. When that happened at Community Church of Joy, it wasn't long before we learned that the real difficulty is not in teaching people how to pray—that's fairly easy. The real difficulty is in building a culture where prayer is second nature because people know from experience that God is among them, engaging them and seeking to be engaged by them. This takes time and patience. It takes changing peoples' worldview from one that accepts only natural explanations for events and has little if any room for a present and active God to one that has room for the divine and assumes the presence and activity of God.

As Michael Foss, pastor of a growing, discipleship-driven congregation in Minnesota, wrote, learning to pray

> is not difficult. We have all learned how to talk to each other. We know how to share our needs with people who care about us and can help us, how to give and receive information, how to ask for things, how to express gratitude, how to say we are sorry and ask for forgiveness, how to say what's important to us and, perhaps most importantly, how to speak words of love and delight to those we love and delight in. And we know how to listen to others when they speak in similar ways to us. Prayer is simply doing what we already know how to do with God as the one to whom we speak and to whom we listen.
>
> The real difficulty is not in learning how to say what's on our hearts and minds—although most of us could stand to brush up on both our self-knowledge and our communication skills. The real difficulty is in creating a context where conversation with God is as natural and to be expected as conversation among families, friends, and acquaintances.[2]

At Community Church of Joy, that's what we set out to do. We talked about prayer. We taught prayer. We prayed. And we kept pointing to the real presence of a listening, loving, calling, and sending God among us. We kept wondering together what this God wanted both for us and from us, and we sought answers in prayer, Bible study, and lively conversation among those who prayed and studied the Bible. Things began to happen:

- Several members of Joy paired off and formed prayer partnerships, thereby giving the discipline of prayer the power of mutual accountability.

- People began dropping into the church in the mornings before going to work for a time of silence and prayer, thus punctuating the day with an awareness of God's presence.

- We began offering regular, practical classes on prayer in our adult education program.

- Seminars on prayer and weekend prayer retreats were added to the schedule and began to broaden our appreciation of the many different methods and practices of prayer in the Christian tradition.

- Prayer vigils were scheduled on a quarterly basis. Both staff and members were invited to pray in rotation twenty-four hours a day for one or two days. Focused prayer on the needs of our larger community flows from these vigils as we pray for schools, teachers, city administrators, students, and police, as well about the tragedies of youth gangs, drugs, promiscuity, and violence, about broken families, wayward kids, and single parents, about the poor and marginalized of our society. Other vigils focus on the needs of Community Church of Joy and its people as in "prayer and supplication" we bring all of our needs before God.

- Every program in the day-to-day life of the church began integrating prayer into its activities. Children and youth, as well as adults, were exposed to the grace-full mystery of prayer, taught to pray, and encouraged to pray.

- The church council adopted the practice of beginning meetings with prayer—for one another as they tackled their responsibilities, for the congregation in its ministry, and for the others whom we had come to see as the real reason for our existence as a Jesus community. The council also developed the practice of interrupting meetings to pray for wisdom and guidance when principled disagreements prevented consensus.

- A prayer team began praying with pastors and worship leaders every Saturday evening and Sunday morning before every service. Other prayer teams began walking through the church praying in classrooms for those who will teach and learn in them, praying in the hospitality center for those who greet and are greeted, praying in the sanctuary for all those who come seeking a word from God, especially for the seekers, for those on the edges of faith.

- At the end of each worship service, a prayer team was assigned to pray with and for any and all who brought concerns and needs to them.

- Prayer teams began to meet during the week to focus on any and all requests for prayer that were received at the church through mail, phone, or drop-in visits.

- Prayer chains were started to involve the larger congregation in the serious prayer needs of our community.

- We determined to enlist 2,000 intercessors by the year 2000 who would commit to praying daily for Community Church of Joy, its ministries, and the others for whom we exist.

With the possible exception of the last one, all of these are steps that any church, regardless of its size, can begin to take. Cumulatively, they begin to create an atmosphere of expectancy, where prayer is natural and where it is just as natural to expect to experience the presence and power of God in and through prayer.

When prayer became our number one priority, a new and holy fire began burning in the lives of our people. At first we looked to prayer to renew, retool, refocus, and revive us, but that's not what happened and it will not happen in any church that takes prayer seriously as the foundational work of mission. The prefix *re* looks to the past, hoping to restore it in the present. Prayer, however, is about now and it is about newness.

God's words of promise to the people of Israel became words of promise to us: "Do not remember the former things, or consider the things of old. I am about to do a new thing; now it springs forth, do you not perceive it? I will make a way in the wilderness and rivers in the desert" (Isaiah 43:18-19). Through the discipline of prayer a Jesus community will not only perceive the new thing God is doing through it, it will begin to live in the reality of that new thing.

As we grew and started adding staff, we decided to hire a full-time staff minister of prayer. Not all congregations can afford to do this. In the early years we couldn't either. Whether it is a volunteer staff person or a salaried staff person, however, it is important to have one person whose only responsibility is to see to it that the community of faith prays. A minister of prayer has three key responsibilities:

- to provide people with opportunities to learn and experience prayer

- to provide structure for the corporate prayer life of the congregation

- to keep continually in front of us the need to be other-centered and not self-centered in our prayer.

A minister of prayer should be a constant reminder to us of what Jesus taught his first followers: "Do not worry, saying, 'What will we eat?' or 'what will we drink?' or 'what will we wear?' For . . . your heavenly Father knows that you need all these things. But strive first for the kingdom of God and his righteousness, and all these things will be given to you as well" (Matthew 6:31-33).

There is no doubt in my mind, heart, and soul that it was our new commitment to be a people of prayer that has brought us this far and will take us further. The intimacy with God that develops through prayer deepens a people's trust and expectation, fosters a healthy interdependence with the divine, and is the ground of a profound joy that sustains us through thick and thin.

There has been much of the "thick and thin" in Joy's experience. For example, when we were in the midst of trying to discern if God wanted us to purchase 200 acres, relocate, and build a major new mission center, the lender we had approached for financing told us that they would be happy to finance us if we were able to independently raise $2 million! If "thick and thin" means "good and bad," that was definitely the thin side of things.

One day as Community Church of Joy's leaders were in my office talking and praying about that seemingly insurmountable goal of $2 million, the telephone rang. It was a trust officer from a local bank, calling to inform me that a 102-year-old client of the bank's had recently died and left a bequest for Joy in her will. He paused for effect and then told me that this woman was a devout Catholic and had never been to Community Church of Joy. Another pause, and he went on to explain that although she had never worshiped at Joy, she had heard stories about what we were doing for children. The needs of children, it seems, were a special passion of hers. Believing that God was working through our church to meet those needs, Gladys Felve left over $2 million for the mission purposes of Joy! I hung up the phone hardly able to speak. The land would be ours. We could begin to build.

Of course, it was not all smooth sailing from then on. We were still in the "thin" of it. Construction was delayed by a costly and time-consuming political struggle with the city's planning and zoning officials. Further serious delays were caused by El Niño rainstorms, and we had to vacate our old facility before the new one was ready for us. We moved to our new campus with no paved parking lots, no electricity, no windows, no doors, no sheetrock, and no sidewalks. The building and grounds were an absolute mess. We prayed every step of the way, drawing strength from the conviction born of intimacy with God that we were not stepping out on a limb alone but that the living God was accompanying us and "all would be well."

We had our critics. There were many in the congregation who did not share the majority vision of a church for others, of a vibrant center for mission whose worship, programs, and resources would be focused outward to reach, to touch, to heal, to include the others all around us. Some of our critics left long before the move to our new location. Others reluctantly came along, but any who were looking for reasons to leave soon found them.

Everything was different. The walk to the worship center from the parking lot took longer. Traffic got heavier. Because of cost overruns, more money needed to be raised than we had expected. The worship center was a large building and less cozy than we were accustomed to. As it filled with the others we were praying for, unfamiliar faces threatened the comfortable familiarity of the "old Joy." We were more spread out, and the sheer size of the campus was overwhelming.

People left and went to other churches. In fact nearly 25 percent of our members left during the transition. We grieved their leaving, but only up to a point. It was sad to see old friends go away and to see many of them leave hurt and angry. Nevertheless, Joy had a new sense of what it meant to be the missionary people of a missionary God, and any who did not and could not share the vision were better off going somewhere else. We said goodbye with sorrow but—in the conviction born through prayer that God had called us to a ministry with and for others—we said goodbye with our faces turned toward the future, not the past.

In spite of losing almost 25 percent of our membership as we moved from being a "maintenance" congregation to being a center for mission, we grew at the same time by close to 40 percent. Prayer releases the presence and power of God into the community of faith through people of faith. This will be disturbing to some and energizing to others.

Unfortunate though it may be, the mission of God to those who are outside the circle of God's blessing draws a line in the sand between those who want the church to be exclusive and those who want the church to be inclusive. God in Christ is on the side of radical inclusivity. We may have a ways to go in achieving the kind of radical inclusivity that God is calling us to, but being committed to growing in that direction is the first and perhaps most important step in getting there.

When Mary and Joseph took the infant Jesus to the Temple, Simeon, "a righteous and devout" man, took the child in his arms and declared, "My eyes have seen your salvation, which you have prepared in the *presence of all peoples*, a light for revelation to the Gentiles. . . ." Then in words that have proven to be all too prophetic, Simeon declared, "This child is destined for the falling and the rising of many in Israel, and *to be a sign that will be opposed*" (Luke 2:29-32, 34). It may seem harsh, but those who would build walls around the church to keep out the "strangers and aliens" in our midst stand in direct opposition to the Jesus who welcomes strangers and aliens into the household of God (Ephesians 2:19).

If Jesus is a "sign that will be opposed," then the church, the body of Christ, the historical presence of Christ incarnated in this time and this place should also be a sign that attracts opposition. Again, we are called to wonder. We who live in a time in which the church largely institutionalizes the values of its surrounding culture and seeks to be conventionally respectable and acceptable need to wonder why we attract so little opposition. Why is our culture largely indifferent to the church and largely dismissive of Christian faith as having little relevance and value in the affairs of the world? Why does the church elicit more in the way of yawns than anger and tolerance than opposition? If we were truly faithful to the crucified one and walked in the ways of the early followers of Christ who were accused of "turning the world upside down," would we be more like light in the darkness and leaven in the loaf than salt that has lost its saltiness? It's worth wondering about. Such wondering takes place in prayer, for prayer is the only way into the heart of God.

First steps to faithfulness in praying for others

Let me suggest a few steps you might take to begin moving your congregation to faithfulness in praying for others:

- *Remember, it begins with leadership.* The pastors, staff, and lay leaders in a congregation must first commit themselves to the discipline of prayer and Bible study if they seriously want it to become the number one priority of the church. Learn and practice the varieties of prayer, and you will be preparing yourself to mentor others in those practices.

- *Pray through God's Word* seeking an understanding of God's will for "those who live in darkness." "If any of you is lacking in wisdom, ask God, who gives to all generously and ungrudgingly, and it will be given you" (James 1:5). Ask for wisdom, faith, courage, and discipline in praying for others, and they will be given to you.

- *Do a prayer inventory.* Analyze the public practices of prayer in the congregation. When do we pray? How do we pray? Who prays? Who and what do we pray for? How do we follow-up our community prayers? A snapshot of your present practices of prayer will position you for positive change.

- *Teach prayer.* Take every opportunity, both formal and informal, to talk about, teach, and practice prayer with the people God has placed into your care and guidance. Be sure to link prayer and Scripture. Teach folks how to pray the Bible and how to read devotionally.

- *Establish a prayer ministry.* Dedicate a volunteer or a salaried staff person to prayer ministry, and let the congregation know that prayer is at the heart of all you do.

- *Set clear goals for your prayer ministry.* Make sure the congregation knows what they are. Make it clear that in prayer we are trying to align ourselves with *God's will* and not trying to bend God to *our will.* It is God's will that we care for each other within the community of faith. It is also God's will that we care deeply for the others who are all around us.

- *Break your goals down* into measurable objectives and your objectives into action plans. Identify the specific prayer-related programs, educational opportunities, and activities you want to begin. Set time lines, assign responsibilities, allocate necessary resources, and determine what your indicators for success should be.

- *Establish an evaluation and quality monitoring system* for your prayer ministry. Right from the beginning, think about how you will evaluate excellence, effectiveness, and efficiency. How will you know when your objectives and goals have been reached? At the end of the day, you need to know if you actually did what you said you would do, and you need to know if what you said you would do was the right thing to do. Careful, honest evaluation gets you ready for the next day. As a result of your evaluation process you will decide (1) to continue what you are doing, (2) to make some key changes in what you are doing to strengthen and improve it, or (3) to abandon what you are doing because it is either ineffective, no longer needed, not driven by your goals, or too great a drain on precious resources of time, talents, and money. Those involved in the various ministries of the church will have their own impressions and feelings about how they are performing and how the ministry is going. It is worth listening to them. Measurable monitoring systems, however, provide objective information for improvements.[3]

Everything begins and ends in prayer

For a Christian, all things begin and end in prayer because all things begin and end in God. It is here that you must begin if you are serious about claiming your community of faith for God and the purposes of God.

As indicated in the first chapter, the decision to become a church for others is a decision to change your individual and communal attitudes and behaviors toward others. Once that decision has been made, the next step is to become a community of prayer and the Word. I would even go so far as to say that if you are not willing to build your personal life and your ministry around prayer, you might as well close this book and read no further. Everything that follows assumes a Jesus community that prays.

Jesus told his followers, "I am the vine, you are the branches. Those who abide in me and I in them bear much fruit, because apart from me you can do nothing" (John 15:5). It is in prayer that we abide in Christ and are open to the mystery of Christ abiding in us. And this leads us inevitably to worship.

Questions to ponder, things to do

• Take a prayer inventory to get a snapshot of the way things are now. When do you pray in your community of faith? How do you pray? Who prays? Who and what do you pray for? How do you follow-up your community prayers? What does this inventory tell you about what you might need to do?

• What opportunities are there in your community of faith for people to learn about how and why and when to pray? Are they adequate for your vision and mission? Are you doing anything to encourage and support both public and private, formal and informal prayer for others?

• Do you require key leaders to commit to being men and women of prayer? If not, what might the barriers to such a requirement be? Do you have a strategy for training leaders in prayer and in being prayer mentors for others?

• List all of the prayer-related activities in your community of faith. Now list prayer-related activities that you would like to add to this list. How many of them are directly related to praying for others? What stands in the way of adding them?

• Do you have a dedicated staff person or volunteer assigned to prayer ministry? If yes, how effective is he/she in educating and leading the community in prayer? Are there any barriers to effectiveness that could be removed? If no, what people do you know who are men and women of prayer that you might ask to begin such a ministry? What could you do to clear the way for such a ministry?

Rejoice always, pray without ceasing,
give thanks in all circumstances;
for this is the will of God in Christ Jesus for you.

—1 Thessalonians 5:16-18

3
Worshiping in a
Church for Others

After the secrets of the unbeliever's heart
are disclosed, that person will bow down
before God and worship him, declaring,
"God is really among you."

—1 Corinthians 14:25

I t is while consciously in the presence of God and in the presence of God's people that we come to know ourselves most deeply. The secrets of our hearts are disclosed, and the secret of God's great *nevertheless love* for us is revealed. This happens in worship when all that we are and all that we yearn to be are brought into God's redeeming presence in the company of a worshiping community.

Remember the story of Susan from the first chapter, the young denizen of the streets, homeless, living from day to day, from man to man, from fix to fix. Remember her first response to worship: "You were talking to me all the time!" The secrets of her heart were disclosed—*to her*—and she began to experience the healing that comes only from God and is made manifest in the caring of a Jesus community.

Worship is the central activity of Christians. It's what we do. We are people who worship precisely because we are the people of God. We belong to God and we know it, and so we

71

come into God's presence together with confidence, bringing praise and thanksgiving. On the one hand, worship is *reverent love and devotion* expressed to the triune God. On the other hand, worship is the ceremonies, prayers, songs, dramas, readings—all the forms through which we together express our reverent love and devotion to the creating, redeeming, and empowering God who has gathered us together in a community of faith and faithfulness.

Crossing the threshold from the secular to the sacred

At its most profound, worship is what a theologian might call a *liminal experience,* a threshold experience. In worship we cross the threshold between ordinary time and sacred time, between ordinary space and sacred space, between the events of daily life and a divine drama in which we have been invited to be one of the players. Good worship helps people psychologically, emotionally, and spiritually to cross the threshold and so ushers them into the presence of God.

Worship is also, unfortunately, one of the greatest bones of contention in the church. Few things exercise the emotions and passions of Christians more than worship! Try to change it on Sunday and your phone will ring off the hook on Monday. Unfamiliar hymns, different musical instruments and styles of music, new liturgical forms, different ways of doing Holy Communion, you name it—changing worship is playing with fire.

But not changing worship may be playing with a worse fire. To insist that nothing in worship be changed, to insist that we keep on doing what we have always done, is finally to reduce worship to magic, to the un-Christian belief that "correct" forms, rituals, and words will somehow compel God to be present "for us."

Of course, magic doesn't work. Forms, rituals, words, and music can never compel God's presence. To use the expression that pioneering psychoanalyst Carl Jung had carved both over the entrance to his house and on his tombstone, "Bidden or not bidden, God is present." God's presence cannot be commanded, it can only be accepted as the gift it is and entered into. Worship helps people do that, and that is why worship has to change as people change.

If there is anything that Community Church of Joy has been most criticized for by mainline Protestants in general and by fellow Lutherans in particular it is our worship. More years ago than I care to remember, worship at Joy was characterized as "entertainment worship." It has become a caricature of what our worship is about that has been difficult to live down.

Do we want our worship to be entertaining? Well, we don't want it to be boring! Listening to music, watching dance and drama, hearing God's word proclaimed—all of this engages people at many different sensory and intellectual levels. Does that mean we treat worship solely as a spectator sport? Not at all. We want those who worship to participate with their bodies, minds, and spirits—as whole people. They sing, pray, read, clap their hands on occasion, participate in Communion, share a friendly greeting with one another, laugh often, and cry often.

To insist that nothing in worship be changed, to insist that we keep on doing what we have always done, is finally to reduce worship to magic.

We are self-consciously a church for others, and so those who criticize our worship often try to box us into the nurture vs. evangelism argument. What is worship about? Is it about nurturing God's people deeper into the faith, or is it about evangelizing those without faith or on the margins of faith? Neither! Worship is about neither nurture or evangelism—it is about encounter.

In worship people encounter God, and God encounters them. In that encounter, faithful people *will be nurtured* and those without faith *will be evangelized*. If worship is about encounter, then the distinction between so-called seekers' worship and believers' worship is a false one.

In *every* worship in a church for others, people of faith join their praise and thanksgiving with the praise and thanksgiving of Christians of every time and every place. That is a nurturing, strengthening, empowering experience of unlimited divine grace. At the same time, in every worship in a church for others, those without faith or on the margins of faith find themselves in a place where "the secrets of [their] hearts are disclosed"; and strangely, wonderfully, they often find themselves bowing "down before God and worship[ing] him, declaring, 'God is really among you.'"

Whether they are Christian or not, in the encounter with God in worship what happens is what needs to happen for all those who have crossed the threshold and come into the presence of God. For each person, what happens to and for them in worship is probably going to be a bit different than what happens for other people simply because we are all unique in our experiences and our needs. In worship the Spirit meets us where we are and invites us to where God would have us be.

Obviously, people of committed faith need to grow in the depth of their understanding and experience of faith. For that reason we provide many opportunities at Community Church of Joy that meet people where they are and provide resources for their continued growth in spiritual depth and maturity. A plethora of Bible studies, small-group experiences, leadership training events, printed, audio, and video resources, mentoring opportunities, and an almost endless list of opportunities for service both in the church and in the larger community create a learning environment where faith and discipleship are taught. A missional community of faith does not depend on worship as the prime opportunity for such growth. Worship, remember, is about encounter.

It is theologically incorrect to argue that people of faith cannot encounter God in Christ and be richly nurtured in worship that is self-consciously welcoming to those who come either without faith or from the margins of faith. This is neither a "dumbing down" of worship nor a reduction of worship to "people-pleasing" entertainment—two things Community Church of Joy has often been accused of. It is worship that welcomes the nonbeliever, along with the believer, into the presence of God.

If we had been content to remain a "church for us," we probably never would have changed our styles and forms of worship—at least not as dramatically as we did. We were fairly comfortable with traditional ways (even if they did seem a bit quaint to many of us), so why change? With our decision to become a church for others, however, change in worship became imperative. Those on the outside were not likely to become comfortable with the traditions of those of us on the inside. Traditional symbols and the language of worship were hard if not impossible to comprehend. The music was "old" and the lyrics in a language that didn't speak to those who hadn't grown up with it. The actions of worship—standing, kneeling, bowing—were awkward for those who didn't know when and how they were supposed to do them.

The gospel is not bound to any form, any ritual, any traditional way of expression. The truth of God's love disclosed in the life and death of Jesus can be expressed and experienced in a bewildering variety of ways. The lessons learned from the global church teach us that. Finding what helps rather than hinders people of this time and this place to cross the threshold into the presence of God is the challenge contemporary worship must grapple with.

The "next church"

In a 1996 *Atlantic Monthly* article, Charles Trueheart wrote about what the impact on worship might be for a church that effectively opens its doors to this generation of nonbelievers.

> No spires. No crosses. No robes. No clerical collars. No hard pews. No kneelers. No biblical gobbledygook. No prayerly rote. No fire, no brimstone. No pipe organs. No dreary eighteenth-century hymns. No forced solemnity. No Sunday finery. No collection plates. This list has asterisks and exceptions, but its meaning is clear. Centuries of European tradition and Christian habit are deliberately being abandoned, clearing the way for new, contemporary forms of worship and belonging. The Next Church, as the independent and entrepreneurial congregations that are adopting these new forms might collectively be called, is drawing lots of people.[1]

Some time ago, my family and I attended Rock Harbor Church in Newport, California. There were no spires or robes or eighteenth-century songs. Trueheart's description of the "next church" perfectly fit this community of faith. The music, messages, and mode of worship were engaging a new generation of people with little or no Christian history. The music was a cross between U2 and Retro. Jeans, T-shirts, and sandals were the uniform of the day. The message spoke to the real lives of real people in language that had been stripped of all religious jargon. Clearly people's lives had been and were being changed, and they worshiped God with the enthusiasm of genuinely thankful people.

Max Lucado gets at what was going on at Rock Harbor by reflecting on a text from Matthew 15:

> "The people," Matthew wrote, "were amazed when they saw the mute speaking, the crippled made well, the lame walking and the blind seeing. . . ." Then Matthew, still

the great economizer of words, gave us another phrase on which I wish he would have elaborated: "They praised the God of Israel." I wonder how they did that? I feel more certain of what they didn't do than of what they did do. I feel confident that they didn't form a praise committee. I feel confident that they didn't sit in rows and stare at the back of each other's heads. I doubt seriously if they wrote a creed on how they were to praise this God they had never before worshiped. I can't picture them getting into an argument over technicalities. I doubt if they felt it had to be done indoors. And I know they didn't wait until the Sabbath to do it. I can imagine throngs of people pushing and shoving. Wanting to get close. Not to request anything or demand anything, but just to say "thank you." However they did it, they did it. And Jesus was touched, so touched that he insisted they stay for a meal before they left. Worship is the "thank you" that refuses to be silenced. We have tried to make a science out of worship. We can't do that. We can't do that anymore than we can "sell love" or "negotiate peace." Worship is a voluntary act of gratitude offered by the saved to the Savior, by the healed to the Healer, and by the delivered to the Deliverer.[2]

There is more than one door into the presence of the holy

The Rock Harbor style of worship is not for everybody, and there is no reason why it should be. It is, however, a style of worship that obviously answers to the spiritual longings of a clearly distinguishable segment of the population. The Christian church taken as a whole needs to provide worship opportunities in many different styles if it is to answer to the spiritual needs of different kinds of people. No church can be—or should try to be—all things to all people. Individual congregations need to choose the style or styles of worship that best serve their missional objectives.

Whom are you trying to reach with the gospel of God's love? What is the context of your local community? What kinds of music, what symbols, what language, what forms of expression make sense and speak to the hearts and spirits of people in that context? These are great questions to struggle with as you seek to design worship that truly invites people into a transforming encounter with God in Christ. A mission-driven struggle with such questions has the power to unbind a tradition-bound church.

With respect to music—which is where the rubber usually hits the road in arguments about worship—there are some people who will be ushered across the threshold into the presence of God by the melodic strains of Bach, and there are other people who will never get there that way. For some, Christian rock will do it, while that same music would keep others far away. For many it may be the throbbing rhythms of any number of ethnic musical traditions that gets them over the threshold, while for still others the haunting, ethereal tones of a Gregorian chant mark the entrance into sacred space and the presence of the divine.

I have hardly begun to list all the musical options that could open the door on the divine for different people in our diverse culture. To believe that the options are limited to "what we have always done" is, again, to reduce worship to magic. It is to worship worship rather than the God who meets us in worship.

A congregation's form of worship and styles of music will inevitably be linked to their understanding of their mission. If a congregation's mission is maintaining the institution for the sake of its members, then its styles of worship and music will likely be exclusive rather than inclusive. If the mission is to participate in God's mission to the world God loves, then worship will seek to draw all people into the circle of God's unconditional, nonjudgmental love. Styles of worship and music will be intentionally welcoming and inclusive.

The distinguishing marks of worship in a church for others

A church for others is not distinguished by its music or its liturgical style, but by its desire to worship in a way that truly invites and welcomes the seekers among us into an encounter with God in Christ. A wide variety of musical styles from country to rock to pop to classical, as well as a wide variety of relevant liturgical forms, can be inviting and welcoming to those with little if any previous experience in Christian worship. Finding the musical style and forms of worship that speak loudly and clearly of God's love in its particular cultural setting is crucial to any church that seeks to be a witness to that love.

Several marks that distinguish the worship of a church for others are helpful to keep in mind as a congregation reflects on its worship in the light of its missionary calling:

- *Worship should always be an experience of reverence for God.* Is our worship done by rote or with the sense that because God is here something is bound to happen? Through words, music, and symbolic action, does our worship communicate an awe-filled sense that we have come into the presence of the creator of heaven and earth? The Letter to the Hebrews proclaimed that, "It is a fearful thing to fall into the hands of the living God" (Hebrews 10:31). Not fear in terms of fright, but in terms of awe, seriousness, wonder, and mystery. If the others among us sense the seriousness with which we take God, they too may begin to take God seriously.

- *Worship should also be an experience of reverence for these others who, like us, are created in the image of God.* Is our worship an experience of grace or judgment? Does it open us to others or close us to them? When asked, "Which commandment is the first of all?" Jesus told those who followed him: "The first is, 'Hear, O Israel: the

Lord our God, the Lord is one; you shall love the Lord your God with all your heart, and with all your soul, and with all your mind, and with all your strength.' The second is this, 'You shall love your neighbor as yourself.' There is no other commandment greater than these" (Mark 12:29-31). Does our worship as clearly communicate our openness to and love for one another and for others as it does our love for God?

- *Worship should be real.* Religious pretense is pretty obvious to people who come in from the outside. Does our worship communicate an impossibly burdensome piety, or does it communicate a humble acknowledgment that our faith is the faith of real people standing in the presence of a forgiving and gracious God with all the problems of real people?

- *Worship needs to be relatable.* What goes on in worship needs to be understandable. The language and symbols of worship need to be drawn from the everyday world of those who worship and not be the private language of some closed, exclusive religious community. Worship needs to be set within a larger cultural frame of reference if it is going to make any sense to newcomers. Can people relate what they hear, see, and do in worship to the world they will return to when the worship hour is over? If not, they will probably not return.

- *Worship must be relevant.* God's love became real in Christ because Christ lived that love among real people, answering to their real needs in the midst of the real world they lived in. Those who come to the church apart from faith are like the folks in Ephesus to whom Paul wrote: "Remember that you were at that time without Christ . . . and *strangers to the covenants of promise, having no hope and without God in the world*" (Ephesians 2:12). Does our worship incarnate Christ in contemporary dress? Does our worship bring hope to people in the midst of the realities they face from day to day—whatever those realities might be—and then send them back into the world *with God*? If not, it is not relevant and will not speak to the strangers among us.

- *Worship is a relational experience.* In worship our relationship with God, our relationships with others, and our relationship with ourselves all need to be taken seriously and need to be tended to. Does our worship draw people closer to God? If so, it will draw people closer to each other. Does our worship draw people closer to each other? If so, it will draw people closer to God. Does our worship build community? If so it will provide a place for people to be accepted, cared for, strengthened, encouraged, healed. That is precisely the kind of authentic community that others are looking for.

- *Worship should resonate with passion.* To be consciously in the presence of the living God should excite strong emotions—emotions of joy and sorrow, of confession and repentance, of hope and yearning. In the book of the prophet Samuel, there is a wonderful story about King David and the people of Israel worshiping with ecstatic music and dancing. David, we are told, "danced before the Lord with all his might. . . . David and all the house of Israel brought up the ark of the Lord with shouting, and with the sound of the trumpet" (2 Samuel 6:14-15). David should be a model for worship leaders, though I suspect that many who lead worship in today's churches would find his behavior scandalous. Too often worship leadership is by rote and routine and it puts people spiritually, if not physically, to sleep. Nothing is more important to worship than the passion of those who lead worship— their passion for God and their passion for God's people. In short, nothing is more important to worship than the *daily encounter* with God in Christ of those who lead worship. In our worship, are newcomers caught up in the passion of God's people for God and in their passion for the people God loves?

- *Finally, worship should be a rewarding experience.* When people head out to the parking lot and head home after worship they should be thinking *and feeling,* "It's a wonderful thing that I was here today." They should feel that the God encountered in worship goes with them back into the lives they lead from day to day. In what ways does our worship add value spiritually, mentally/emotionally, and physically to those who bring themselves, their needs, and dreams into the presence of God? Those on the edges of faith who cross the threshold into our churches must be able to take something with them when they re-cross the threshold back to the parking lot. An experience, a thought, a feeling, a practice that flows from having encountered God as they are, who they are, and where they are. When this happens, people return because they can't stay away.

Bringing worship back to the center

Planning worship and then worshiping are two of the most important things that happen in a church for others. Worship is the heartbeat of a Jesus community. You cannot take it too seriously because it is only in the encounter with God that lives can be changed. Worship is the seedbed of personal transformation.

Worship planning and worship leadership should not be left only to the clergy, an organist, or a choir director. Worship is too important to rely solely on the gifts of only one or two people. Every church, regardless of its size, needs a worship planning team. At Community Church of Joy, our worship planning team is staff-driven. In a smaller church a worship planning team will most likely be volunteer-driven.

Whether staff-driven or volunteer-driven, what is important is to have a dedicated group of people who take it as their mission to:

- ensure that each worship service reflects all the marks of worship set forth above

- engage as many people in up-front worship roles as possible

- educate the people of God as to the meaning of worship so that everybody knows what we do and why we do it

- continually evaluate the effectiveness of worship in the congregation's missionary task of inviting people into an encounter with God

- consult with program leadership to ensure that worship themes and program themes relate to each other.

One of the first things a worship planning team should do is craft a mission statement that lets the members of the team—and the members of the congregation—know precisely what they are about. A good mission statement says who you are, what you do, and what outcomes you are committed to. Generic mission statements don't work. People have to struggle through to a statement that makes sense to them in the context of their own ministry if the mission statement is to truly guide them in their worship planning. Mission statements should be short, easily memorized, and constantly referred to in the planning process.

An effective statement might look something like this:

> *The Worship Team plans worship that (1) invites all people into the presence of the triune God, (2) honors both God and the "others" we seek to serve in God's name, (3) proclaims the gospel with a clarity that is*

relevant and relatable to our culture, and (4) uses the
gifts of many so that God is truly worshiped, Christ is
truly known, and all people are truly empowered by the
Spirit to follow him.

Worship that keys off the mission statement will be worship
that embodies the community's vocation as a church for others. By testing worship ideas against the mission statement,
worship planners are encouraged to keep their missionary
focus and not lose sight of the others who on any given Sunday might cross the threshold into the church and thus into
the presence of God.

Worship planning teams should hold planning retreats at
least twice a year to lay out plans for the next six months of
worship. Planning six months at a time gives long-range
focus, continuity, and consistency to worship planning, as
well as an opportunity to correlate worship themes with what
will be going on in the ongoing programs of the church. Fine-
tuning can take place along the way, but a careful six-month
plan for worship ensures that worship is never done in a
random fashion. It keeps everybody on the same page and
gives plenty of time for recruiting worship participants, preparation, and practice.

The six-month plan is implemented in weekly meetings of
the planning team. First the team studies together a worship-
related scriptural text and then prays together for all those
who plan and participate in worship and for all those who will
attend. The wisdom of God and the power of the Spirit are
sought both to strengthen the faith of believers and to bring
to faith those who are "far off."

Next the elements of worship for the following several
weeks are determined. These might include the thematic flow
of the service, the message, choral or special music, video
testimonies, drama and/or dance, holy communion and/or
baptism. Assignments of responsibility for each of the elements of worship are made, and recruitment needs for worship participants are discussed. Any special technical needs

are noted and arranged for. These might include visuals, sound system, or lighting. Special attention is paid to the way the various elements of the service interact with each other. Care is taken to ensure that each element supports and is supported by every other component in the worship service so that a unified message is presented and reinforced.

Throughout, planning team members ask themselves, "Is this an 'other-friendly' worship?" Toward this end, the worship planning team prepares, distributes, collects, and analyzes periodic and random evaluations of worship by both members and nonmembers. The goal is to discover how worship is experienced by all who cross the threshold into the sacred space of the worship center. Without such an understanding, the attempt to be both relevant and relatable in worship can easily miss the mark.

Depending on the complexity of the worship being planned and the nature of the worship elements being integrated in the service, both separate and collective rehearsals might be called for. Choirs, praise bands, and special music ensembles will normally rehearse each week, as will drama and dance teams. Technical people need to run through their cues and test-run visuals. On occasion, bringing everybody together for a complete rehearsal may be necessary. What is important is to express through careful preparation the seriousness with which worship is taken.

Worship is worship, not performance

The danger, of course, is that worship can all too easily be reduced to technique—a controlled experience seeking controlled results. The danger can and *must be guarded against.*

- Of first importance is the need simply to be aware of the danger, to be aware of the powerful temptation to usurp the freedom of the Spirit with the control of human technique.

- Of second importance is the humility to ask God to protect you from that temptation and the grace to be self-critical.

- Of third importance is the spiritual focus of those who lead and/or have roles in the various elements of worship.

If those who lead or have a role to carry out in worship understand themselves essentially as performers, the problem emerges. If they experience themselves as people *who are themselves in worship* and not in performance, as people encountering the mystery of God in the face of Christ, as people whose gifts proclaim the glory of God and not their own glory, as people in a divine drama scripted by God, the danger can be avoided.

It is of paramount importance that those involved with worship planning keep the dangers of a performance mentality before them. Talk about it. Pray about it. Encourage one another in the spiritual disciplines that dispose Christians to true worship and gently hold each other accountable for attitudes and behaviors that might make the worship team a barrier standing between those who cross the threshold and the God who waits to encounter them in worship.

Variety can be the spice of life

A final word about styles of worship. Worship services can seek either breadth or narrowness. They can either appeal to as broad a segment of the population as possible or appeal to a tightly targeted segment of the population. In a church for others, decisions about worship and music styles will always relate to the missionary calling of the church. Whom is God calling you to reach in your particular community with its particular problems and possibilities?

Smaller congregations will normally want to choose a primary style of worship. They will want to choose music that is both intergenerational and meets the needs of as broad a spectrum of people as possible. Where the situation permits more than one worship service a weekend, rather than have two identical services, targeting a specific group in the additional service will extend the reach of the congregation.

As we have grown at Community Church of Joy, we have added worship services that maximize our ability to provide worship experiences that respond to an increasingly diverse cultural reality. Our primary services are large, intergenerational gatherings where we seek breadth of participation. In addition we have a more traditional service where the language of worship has been contextualized but the forms and music of worship draw heavily from the richness of Christian traditions of years if not centuries past. We have weekly worship for singles, where worship planning focuses on the unique needs and concerns of the unmarried. We have weekly youth worship, where worship planning takes with great seriousness the interests, needs, and perspectives of the kids in Generation Y.

Many of these services meet simultaneously with our larger services in other locations on our campus. With our commitment to worship as the heart of Christian life and mission, we feel as if we have just begun. The challenges are immense and exciting. As much as we would like to, we can't do everything at once. Limitations of human and financial resources compel us to follow incremental patterns of growth. As we continue to grow, and as our resources grow with us, our horizons expand before us:

- As our senior center grows we will provide worship opportunities that center on the spiritual concerns unique to those in their later years of life.

- Worship that speaks in both form and music to the uniqueness of diverse ethnic and cultural groups, such as the increasing population of Latinos and the indigenous Native American peoples, commends itself to us as a church for others located in Arizona.

- Worship that engages the disadvantaged and disenfranchised of our society to encounter the liberating power of God through Scripture, proclamation, and music read, spoken, and sung in the midst of the harsh realities of their lives is something we have barely begun to think about but which lies on our horizon as a challenge from our missionary God.

The argument has been made that our increasing size and increasing diversity of worship opportunities has turned us from a single church into a collection of disparate congregations. I suppose that's somewhat true, but I don't see the problem. We understand ourselves as a unified community consisting of many sub-communities. What unifies us is our common vision and missionary commitment to be a church for others. We are relentless in our common commitment to be a part of God's mission to the world God loves.

We often see *cross-pollination*—people who primarily worship in a particular service occasionally worship with other groups. They are encouraged to reflect on their experience and to wonder if anything they experienced could help to enrich the worship of their primary group. And regardless of which service a person worships at, everyone is encouraged to participate in the wide variety of educational, service, and social programs that cut across every discrete worshiping group.

What might be called *affinity worship* facilitates the encounter with God for people with common experiences, interests, backgrounds, goals, and needs. That finally is what matters. In a large and growing church for others, expanding the range of worship opportunities is a mission imperative in the increasingly diverse and pluralistic culture of the United States. In our variety of worship opportunities, we are trying to understand and emulate what Paul said when he wrote, "I have become all things to all people, that I might by all means save some. I do it all for the sake of the gospel" (1 Corinthians 9:22b-23a).

Proclaiming the mighty acts of God

Worship in a church for others is rooted in the conviction that God has gathered us together for a purpose—to draw all people into the light of God's unfailing love. We do not worship for ourselves alone, although we are ourselves deeply nourished in worship. We worship as people with a mission. A church for others echoes the sentiments of St. Paul: "If I proclaim the gospel, this gives me no ground for boasting, for an obligation is laid on me, and woe to me if I do not proclaim the gospel!" (1 Corinthians 9:14). It is what we are called to do. It is our vocation—individually as Christians and together as a community of faith.

Peter characterized the missionary people of God beautifully when he wrote: "But you are a chosen race, a royal priesthood, a holy nation, God's own people, *in order that you may proclaim* the mighty acts of him who called you out of darkness into his marvelous light" (1 Peter 2:9).

As people who live in that "marvelous light," we can do no other than to invite all people out of the darkness—and to make the invitation as inviting as possible!

Questions to ponder, things to do

• Sit in the pew and ponder your worship services. What would a seeker see, hear, do? Would it all make sense? Would he or she understand the language, rituals, and routines of worship?

• How is worship planning done now? Who does it? Who are the worship "gatekeepers" in your community who would need to be convinced before change in worship could be implemented?

• Reread the eight characteristics of worship in a church for others on pages 79–82. Now analyze your worship in terms of these marks of worship in a church sensitive to the presence of seekers. Does your worship reflect each of these eight characteristics? What does your analysis tell you about what needs to be done?

• Reread the worship team mission statement on pages 83–84. Now, working with worship planners in your congregation, craft a mission statement to guide you in planning worship.

• As you think about the larger social/cultural context where you live, are their any particular populations that your mission to others suggests you should develop specific worship services for? What would first steps be in developing such a service? Who should be involved with you in the planning? What barriers do you face? How can they be overcome?

Be filled with the Spirit,
as you sing psalms and hymns and
spiritual songs among yourselves,
singing and making melody to the
Lord in your hearts. . . .
—Ephesians 5:18b-19

4

Proclaiming the Gospel in a Church for Others

Everyone who calls on the name of the
Lord shall be saved.
But how are they to call on one in whom
they have not believed?
And how are they to believe in one of whom
they have never heard?
And how are they to hear without someone
to proclaim him?
                              —Romans 10:13-14

Late one Saturday night, while I was putting the final touches on the message I planned to deliver the next morning, I decided to drive up to the church and sit for a while in the chairs that my congregation would be occupying in just a few hours' time. As I sat in the dimly lit sanctuary, facing the pulpit and enfolded in silence, I began reflecting on the outline, the stories, and the content of my message. In that solitary moment, as I sat alone with my thoughts in the presence of God, it dawned on me that I had very little to say to any who might enter the church tomorrow either without faith or from the far margins of faith—nothing to say to those others that the Spirit might lead across the threshold.

91

Everything I had planned to say was for insiders, for faithful, mature believers. The theological and religious language I had planned on using was jargon—clear to insiders and gibberish to outsiders. The assumptions about biblical familiarity I had made were sweeping and would leave those with no Christian memory in the dust. None of my illustrations included the experiences and questions of those with no faith or those who were living on the edges of faith. There was nothing bad or heretical about my message. It probably would have been well-regarded in a seminary sermon-preparation class. It just wouldn't have touched the real hurts and sorrows, the real needs, the real yearnings, dreams, and hopes of others.

In the silence of that night I wondered: "How are *they—the others in our midst—* to hear without someone to proclaim him *to them?*" It was a sobering question and I drove back home through the darkened streets still wondering. Before finally laying my head on the pillow that night, I resolved to begin bringing the word of God to all who crossed the threshold into the church in ways that *do not leave anyone out.*

A word of God for everyone

Let me repeat—in ways that do not leave *anyone* out. Churches such as Community Church of Joy that intentionally seek the "seekers" are often criticized for dumbing down the gospel, for lacking depth, for failing to meet the needs of the faithfull in their eagerness to meet the needs of the faith-less. But that is not the case. Simplicity and clarity of expression, everyday language, symbols drawn from contemporary culture, illustrations taken from the streets, homes, boardrooms, marketplaces, factories, and schools where people actually live their lives cannot be equated with either dumbing down the gospel or shallowness. They equate rather with relevance and relatability, and such things are as necessary for the faithful as they are for those who know little if anything about the faith.

The gospel is simple: God, in and through Jesus, saves us because God loves us and not because of what we do or don't do. Having saved us, God calls us to live lives with each other that mirror God's love for us.[1] It is simple and yet profound in its implications. A message that draws those implications out in ways that are understandable, compelling, and challenging to people with little or no Christian faith will speak just as clearly and compellingly to people of faith.

My friend Mike Foss draws an apt illustration from another religious tradition. "In Zen Buddhism," he writes, "even experienced practitioners are admonished to maintain a 'beginner's mind.' The humility, openness, simplicity, and eagerness to learn of the beginner are qualities that should not be lost with time and experience."[2] His point is well taken. It is in hearing the gospel again and again, in all of its simplicity, with a "beginner's mind" that one experiences the wisdom and power of Christ for true transformation.[3] Any believer who comes to a so-called seekers' service with the humility of a beginner's mind and with the expectation that he or she will hear a word from God will hear a word from God.

It is also good to remember that the sermon or message is but one of the elements of worship. When all the elements of worship work together to create an environment where God can be truly encountered, the power of the simplest message to touch deeply the hearts and minds of all *in the way they need to be touched* is released in wonderfully unpredictable ways.

The ten commandments of communication

Over the years I have developed ten guidelines for proclaiming the gospel in a church for others. Although especially helpful in crafting weekly worship messages that effectively and faithfully proclaim God's truth in ways that are accessible to any and all who might be there, these guidelines can be useful to anyone who teaches in the church in any capacity.

It is worth noting that although on the printed page things have to be presented one after the other, the ten commandments of communication do not represent a linear process. It is a dynamic process. The different guidelines interact and overlap, often go on simultaneously, and circle around each other. The ten commandments of communication can be summarized simply:

- Know what you teach.
- Live what you teach.
- Know whom you teach.
- Love whom you teach.

The first commandment—You shall prepare

It was said of the prophet Hezekiah that "every work that he undertook in the service of the house of God, and in accordance with the law and the commandments, to seek his God, he did with all his heart; and he prospered" (2 Chronicles 31:21). All Christian leaders want to prosper in every work that they undertake "in the service of the house of God." Tragically, however, many do not prosper. They feel ineffective, inadequate, burned out, and used up. After four or five years of preaching Sunday after Sunday, all too many pastors complain of having nothing more to say. After teaching Sunday school or confirmation classes or adult Bible studies year after year, all too many Christian leaders are as bored with it as those who come to learn from them. As one burned-out and used-up pastor put it, "I can't blame people for falling asleep during the sermon when it's all I can do to stay awake myself!"

What can be done about this? There is a clue in this text from 2 Chronicles. In "every work that he undertook in the service of the house of God" Hezekiah did it with "all of his heart." He prepared well and executed well. Nothing less is asked of us. But that is not all that he did with all his heart. It seems that "in accordance with the law and the commandments" he also sought God with all his heart. Whatever one does to seek God is also preparation. *Indeed, the foundational preparation for any kind of ministry is to seek God with all your heart.*

To prosper "in the service of the house of God," then, two kinds of preparation are necessary for Christian leaders:

- The *foundational* preparation of seeking God with all your heart.
- The *executable* preparation for specific ministry tasks, also done with all your heart.

Effective and faithful ministry needs both kinds of preparation, and the Christian leader who avoids either of them does so at his or her own peril. All ministry is rooted in the disciplines of prayer, Bible study, and theological reflection that seek God. And specific tasks of ministry—the Sunday message, the youth retreat, premarriage counseling, the soup kitchen—all depend on intensive task-specific preparation and skillful execution.

Let's apply this to proclaiming the gospel in a church for others. Before any worship leader can ever expect effectively and faithfully to speak a word of God into the life circumstances of those who come to worship, he or she has to be thoroughly immersed in the word of God in his or her own life circumstances. Effective Christian leaders live in and out of the word of God. It is what enables them to bring that word into the lives of others.

The essential daily checklist for those who proclaim the gospel looks like this:

- Daily Bible study
- Daily devotions and prayer
- Daily theological study in the context of your time and place

This checklist is the *sine qua non*, that which is essential to ministry—be it ordained ministry or lay ministry. The

Bible, prayer, theological reflection—these are the well-springs from which Christian leaders drink to slake their own thirst for God, and from which they draw to slake the thirst of others.

For the specific task of delivering a specific message on any given Sunday, careful preparation begins with immersion in the word of God that forms the heart of the message. Soak yourself in the Scripture. Read it over and over and over again. In short, memorize it. Struggle with it. Don't ever presume to tell others what it means for them until you have wrestled with it long enough to know what it means for you. As the writer to the Hebrews exclaimed, "Indeed, the word of God is living and active, sharper than any two-edged sword, piercing until it divides soul from spirit, joints from marrow; it is able to judge the thoughts and intentions of the heart" (Hebrews 4:12). Once the word of God has judged the thoughts and intentions of your own heart, you will be prepared to speak this living and active word into the lives of others.

Finally, with respect to preparation, no one would try to make a piece of fine pottery without patiently mastering the potter's craft. Regardless of the craft, mastering the appropriate skills and tools is fundamental to creative expression. Powerful and persuasive public speaking is no different. It is an art. It has necessary skills and tools. They can be learned, developed, honed—and must be. We would have little tolerance for a cardiac surgeon who was not expert in the tools of her trade. What is at stake in her level of expertise—the lives of those under her care—is too great. We should have no more tolerance for those who bring God's word to the people God loves Sunday after Sunday who are not expert in the tools of their trade. What is at stake—the lives of those who come to hear—is just as great.

The second commandment—
You shall enter the world outside the church

In the early years of her career, popular Christian singer Amy Grant recorded and performed her music largely within and for the Christian world. In the late 1980s, she "crossed over" and began recording and performing her music within and for the secular world. It was a principled decision that outraged many Christians who thought that she had sold out. At a concert in Cincinnati, she explained to the hushed crowd why she had made the decision to bring her wonderful gift of music into the world outside the church:

> Some think I should stand in the light and give my witness. But I believe God has called me to stand in the dark, and there give off my light. I know there is danger in the dark, but God's Word has told me that I'm all right as long as I don't loose sight of the light.[4]

The night before he was crucified for love of the world, Jesus prayed to God about and for his followers. "As you have sent me into the world," he prayed, "so I have sent them into the world" (John 17:18). Not into the church, not into the sanctuary or the cloister—into the world.

Many years ago a respected seminary president argued that seminary interns shouldn't be "little pastors" who play church for a year and then return safely to the academic ivory tower. It seems he believed that the best internship would be for them to work in a factory or drive a cab.

Jesus, Amy Grant, and this seminary president have something in common—a deep love and respect for those on the outside of the religious establishment. If you are going to invite such folks to cross the threshold into the community of faith, you need to know the world they are coming from.

There are, of course, many ways to enter the world outside the church, but they all boil down to two methods. You can either enter the world outside the church vicariously or personally. Those who proclaim the gospel should do both.

To enter vicariously is to enter through the experience of others.

- Read voraciously. Consume as many nonreligious newspapers, magazines, and books as you have time for. They will keep you current and up-to-date on the issues, concerns, interests, fads, habits, and trends that affect the lives of those you are seeking to draw into the circle of God's love. If you are seeking to reach a specific group of people, read what they read. For example, no one should seriously try to relate to the unchurched elderly without regularly reading the American Association of Retired Persons (AARP) magazine, *Modern Maturity*. If you want to reach Generation Next, read *Rolling Stone*. If you want to draw a particular ethnic group across the threshold, read their literature, their magazines, their newspapers.

- Watch TV. Go to the movies. Listen to music. The values that shape this generation, the fears that threaten this generation, the hopes that move this generation, and the myriad of problems that unsettle this generation are all there, reflected on the tube, the screen, in the lyrics.

To enter personally is to go on your own two feet and experience the world outside the church yourself.

- Go to shopping malls, coffee shops, bars, parks, the beach—wherever people gather—and strike up conversations. Ask good questions that open you to the experiences of the folks you meet, to their reality, and then just listen. Ask follow-up questions to increase understanding and then just listen.

- Make appointments with government officials, union leaders, teachers, police officers, social workers, crisis centers, prison officials, local artists. Ask good questions and then just listen. Every overseas missionary knows that the first thing you need when you enter a new culture is "cultural informants," people who know the cultural landscape and can teach you what you need to know.

- Develop friendships with people who are not Christian. Don't let your only purpose be their conversion, rather simply seek to enter their world, earn their trust, and enjoy them at the same time you give them your trust and let them enjoy you.

- Join non Christian organizations. Serve on the school board, work in a soup kitchen, or join a non-church-related social group. You know of my love for motorcycles. Some time ago I was inducted into the Glendale Hog Club for Harley Davidson owners. I joined because I own a Harley and I want to understand the world that other motorcycle lovers live in. Those who proclaim the gospel should follow their interests into non-Christian groups. Join the civic and social gatherings of your community and then observe, ask questions, and listen.

You can't effectively communicate the gospel of God's love unless you know the context within which you are communicating. Those who proclaim the Christian message in a church for others need to be experts on the local, regional, and national culture. Those who would proclaim the gospel to others need to immerse themselves both vicariously and personally in the experiences of contemporary culture for the sake of understanding that culture. Without such empathic understanding it will be difficult if not impossible to relate God's word and the Christian life of faith to those who don't yet know them.

The third commandment—
You shall make the connection

If you rigorously follow the first two commandments, you will find yourself living consciously in the presence of God, immersed in God's word, and immersed in the larger world outside the walls of the church. What comes next is simply to make the connection between the word and the world, between the real, nitty-gritty lives of real people and the real God who loves them. The Sunday message flows out of the speaker's encounter with God and the world. It proclaims the connection between God's truth and the nuts and bolts of daily life. Its focus is not on God's truth or on the nuts and bolts. It is on the connection between them. Despite their value, it is not theological or biblical studies but your own personal religious authenticity that makes the connection. No amount of psychological understanding or self-help tips can substitute for your own insight into God's word connected to the concrete life circumstances of real people.

The fourth commandment—
You shall be transparent

Tim Wright, the executive pastor at Community Church of Joy, has had problems with anxiety. There was a time in his life when overwhelming panic attacks practically paralyzed him. Then one weekend, as Tim was delivering his message to those who had gathered for worship, he choose to become transparent. He openly told those in attendance about his personal battle with anxiety and then made the connection between his fear and his faith. He spoke of how he experienced grace in the midst of anxiety and found the courage to struggle with his problem in the confidence that God was with him in the struggle. His transparency had a profound impact on those fortunate enough to hear him. Many of those present that day were fighting similar battles with anxiety and fear. In Tim's vulnerability, they discovered the possibility of hope in the midst of their own pain.

How many Christians over the centuries have drawn comfort and strength from St. Paul's transparency when he confessed that he too had a "thorn in the flesh"?

> Three times I appealed to the Lord about this, that it would leave me, but he said to me, "My grace is sufficient for you, for power is made perfect in weakness." So, I will boast all the more gladly of my weaknesses, so that the power of Christ may dwell in me. Therefore I am content with weaknesses, insults, hardships, persecutions, and calamities for the sake of Christ; for whenever I am weak, then I am strong (2 Corinthians 12:8-10).

Suddenly, in his transparency, the great apostle becomes human to us, one of us, someone we can relate to. He gives us hope when we see how in the midst of a seemingly intractable problem he draws strength and courage from the God who loves him. If Paul can do it, so can we.

Transparency can be dangerous. The danger lies in the temptation to focus the message on yourself rather than on the Christ whose grace is sufficient for you. There is also a danger in not being transparent. Here the danger lies in losing the listener. The people who enter the church seeking meaning, faith, purpose, hope, or help need to relate to both the message and the messenger. If the messenger comes across as a religious superhero, or as having his or her act completely together, the astute seeker will not believe it and most likely will not cross the threshold again. Above all, the seekers in our midst are looking for authenticity. Those who proclaim the gospel in a church for others, confident that God is a forgiving, merciful, compassionate God, will risk the vulnerability that comes with being transparent for the sake of authenticity and integrity.

The fifth commandment—
You shall let your convictions show

Paul, a man clearly driven by his passion for bringing the good news of Christ to nonbelievers, wrote to those he had helped cross the threshold into the body of Christ, "For we know, brothers and sisters beloved by God, that he has chosen you, because our message of the gospel came to you not in word only, but also in power and in the Holy Spirit *and with full conviction*" (1 Thessalonians 1:4-5). Convictions have to do with walking the talk, with living the truth that you proclaim. Paul translated the gospel into action and in so doing convinced others of the truth of the gospel.

Convictions lived out consistently in the give-and-take of daily life have tremendous persuasive power. A lack of strong convictions, or voiced convictions that are invalidated by or even contradicted by behavior, reinforce the conventional wisdom that religion is little more than a mask for hypocrisy.

If you are going to speak about forgiveness, you need to practice forgiveness. If you are going to encourage tithing, you need to tithe. If you are going to proclaim love, you need to be loving. The others in our midst who listen to our proclamations will quickly see through the façade if there is a façade to see through. Speaking on Sunday is not just a matter of speaking on Sunday. It is a matter of the faith-based convictions that inform the way you live. Mahatma Gandhi said it with remarkable clarity:

> The things that will destroy us are:
> Politics without principle,
> Pleasure without conscience,
> Wealth without work,
> Knowledge without character,
> Business without morality,
> Science without humanity,
> And worship without sacrifice.[5]

In Jesus "the Word became flesh and lived among us" (John 1:14), and for 2,000 years we have been trying to turn that flesh back into words. It won't work. The words spoken on Sunday morning will finally be meaningless and empty of power if those who proclaim them do not *struggle to incarnate their truth*. The person seeking authenticity in the church will be attracted by the struggle but will be repelled if the words he or she hears on Sunday are shown to mask a life without conviction.

Of course, in a church for others, the primary conviction that drives the preacher from Monday to Saturday and resonates in his or her words on Sunday is the conviction that God is radically inclusive and expects the community of faith to be just as radically inclusive. The church is the church for others or it is not the church of Jesus Christ.

Much of the malaise in today's Protestantism comes from the fact that too many preachers see as their primary task simply sending people home feeling good about themselves. If offending no one is the preacher's goal, will not he or she either enlighten anyone. There are times when our individual and corporate sinfulness needs to be challenged. Preaching that is rooted in faith-based convictions will have the courage to say what a congregation may not want to hear but needs to hear. I'm not talking about heaping guilt on people or the kind of carping criticism that belittles and diminishes people. I am talking about the courage to say, with a conviction expressed in the way you live, "We have heard it said . . . but Jesus says to us. . . ."

The sixth commandment—You shall be practical

Hard memories are sometimes the best, for hard experiences are the ones we learn from. Let me share one of mine. A middle-aged man walked up to me after the service, shook my hand, and said, "Pastor, is Christianity practical?"

"Well, of course," I said.

"And do you try to make your sermons practical?"

"Of course," I said again.

"Well," he said with a smile. "For me, practical means when I leave I have something to do."

"OK"

"And today," he continued, "I don't have anything to do."

No one should ever leave church with nothing to do. Whether people come with faith or with little or no faith, they come needing transformation. The encounter with God is an invitation to transformation. Jesus told those who followed him:

> Therefore everyone who hears these words of mine and puts them into practice is like a wise man who built his house on the rock. The rain came down, the streams rose, and the winds blew and beat against that house; yet it did not fall, because it had its foundation on the rock. (Matthew 7:24-25)

Those who come to church for the first time ever or for the first time in a long time normally come because they want life to be different and they wonder—sometimes desperately—if Christian faith can help them. Remember Doug, whose story I told in the first chapter—the man in the throes of a painful divorce, ready to kill himself, who came to church and gave us one chance to be real, accepting, helpful, and practical.

Every time you prepare a message for a weekend worship service think it through from the perspective of those who will hear it and ask yourself, "What will they have to do on Sunday afternoon, and on Monday, and on Tuesday, and . . . ?" This has nothing to do with legalism, with piling new burdens on those who are already heavily burdened. It has everything to do with spiritual guidance, spiritual formation, with helping people begin to practice—and thus experience—grace as power for living.

The seventh commandment— You shall use your imagination

While flipping through a magazine on an airplane, I came across a Microsoft advertisement that immediately grabbed my attention:

> Wouldn't it be cool if your computer could . . . ?
> Well, if somebody can imagine it,
> chances are your computer will someday do it.
> Amazing things. Useful things. Silly things.
> And of course, this says more
> about people than it does about computers.
> People are born to innovate, invent, and create. . . .

It could be said that the playground of the soul is the imagination. A good message engages the imagination of the speaker and the listener. Together they can see the world as it is, imagine it as God would have it, and then wonder together about ways to bridge the gap. The message should engage people in an imaginative venture that leads to both personal transformation and the transformation of the whole community of faith.

Ask yourself what the biblical reading at the heart of your message implies for the way the world should be, the way people should be, the way the church should be. Ask yourself what the Bible implies about the resources of faith and grace, of individuals, and of the community as resources for transformation. Ask yourself what the Scriptures proclaim about the living God, and what hope, courage, strength, and endurance people can claim because of who God is and what God does. And then wonder with those who have come to hear what it all means in the concrete, often hard realities that they face from day to day.

If you have been following these ten commandments of communication you will know quite a bit about those realities and, because you will have been living both in God's word and in the world outside the church, you will have plenty of fuel to fire your imagination and the imaginations of those who privilege you with their attention.

The eighth commandment—
You shall be enthusiastic

In the book of Acts we read about an early Christian named Apollo. "He had been instructed in the Way of the Lord; and he spoke with burning enthusiasm and taught accurately the things concerning Jesus" (Acts 18:25). It is an apt description of how everyone who stands in front of people to proclaim God's truth ought to be: wise in the Way of the Lord, focused on Jesus, and speaking with burning enthusiasm.

It is interesting to note that the English noun *enthusiasm* comes from the Greek noun *enthousiasmos*, a derivative of the Greek adjective, *entheos*, which means "having the god within."[6] To be enthusiastic literally means *to be filled with God!*

Once again we are faced with an unavoidable truth—all ministry is rooted in the spirituality of those who do ministry, ordained or lay. Those who proclaim the gospel in a church for others must do it out of their own relationship with God, not out of textbooks or commentaries, not by cutting and pasting together illustrations from an Internet sermon marketplace or mall. Enthusiasm does not come from borrowing. Boredom comes from borrowing. Enthusiasm comes from the encounter with God.

In Ephesians we are admonished: "Render service with enthusiasm, as to the Lord and not to men and women" (Ephesians 6:7). Your love, compassion, and care for the men and women who cross the threshold of your church are certainly important and even necessary, but they are not sufficient. Love, compassion, and caring people can be found outside the church. What the seekers in our midst are looking for and can find nowhere else is the gospel of God's love for them. In a church for others, people will come again and again, like moths to a light, if they sense your enthusiasm, your passion, your love for God. It's what they want for themselves. They will take your enthusiasm, passion, and love for God as a sign that it's all real, and all possible, possibly even for them.

The ninth commandment— You shall "ask for the order"

My friend Paul Schrage, who helped develop McDonald's into the fast-food giant it is today, once said to me, "One of the most important things we do is ask for the order. I think that what's missing in most Christian churches and organizations is that we never ask for the order. People come week after week, month after month, and year after year and we never get around to asking for the order."[7]

If someone goes into a restaurant hungry and thirsty and no one ever asks for their order, they will leave and not return. If those outside the church come inside the church hungering and thirsting for God, seeking healing, looking for meaning and purpose, and no one ever "asks for their order," they will leave and not return.

Would you like a relationship with God? Would you like to know Christ? Would you like fullness of life now and after death? Would you like to be a disciple of Christ? Would you like to live in the power of the Spirit? In one way or another, the messages that people come to hear on Sunday have to address these and similar questions. The proclamation of the good news of Jesus Christ always includes an invitation—the invitation to follow him, to live in and through him. The proclamation of the gospel in a church for others has to be explicit about both the salvation that is freely given in Jesus and the invitation to follow Jesus now.

The others who cross the threshold are not interested in salvation if it is largely a "pie in the sky by and by" kind of salvation. They want a life now that makes sense. They are looking for an experience of transcendence that transforms everyday emptiness into fullness of life. They are looking for God. Take their order.

The tenth commandment— You shall evaluate

The only ones who can tell you how you are doing are those who give you the privilege of speaking to them. If you don't know how they hear you and what they are hearing, you are speaking into a vacuum. Evaluation can come in many forms:

- Have yourself videotaped while you speak and then watch the tape and debrief with trusted colleagues. Try it occasionally with randomly selected folks who sat there and listened to you.

- Hold separate focus groups of randomly selected newcomers and old-timers following worship and talk frankly about both style and content of the message. Ask folks what they heard and how they felt about it.

- Have ushers randomly hand out short written questionnaires and a pencil after each service. Ask the folks to fill it out before they leave. Ask questions that let you know if their "order" was taken, and if they "have something to do" as a result of having listened.

Take seriously the feedback you get. It may be hard to hear. You may feel it is unfair, inaccurate, and not worth the time you took to get it. But remember, it is from the people you hope will genuinely hear, understand, and respond to what you say. Let them help you speak in ways they can hear.

Perhaps nothing we do in the church is finally more important to those outside the church than the time we spend preparing to speak—and speaking—the word of God. It is tragic that we burden pastors with so much busyness that the proclamation of the gospel gets short shrift in overburdened schedules. "There just isn't time to prepare really well!" is a complaint that I hear again and again from pastors who are at the end of their tether. If a church that has decided to be a church for others could afford it, they should have a person or team on the staff whose *only job* is to proclaim the good news of God's love in Jesus Christ "with burning enthusiasm." It's a full-time job, and there is none more important.

Questions to ponder, things to do

(Although these questions are directed at those who bring the message in worship, it would be a good exercise to discuss them with the key leadership of the congregation and/or the worship planning team.)

• Sit in the chairs your people sit in Sunday after Sunday. Think about your next message and "listen" to it with the ears of someone new to the church. Will they be able to understand you? Do you need to make any changes in your language or illustrations? Does your style of presentation aid or inhibit understanding?

• An authentic message comes from the speaker's own ongoing encounter with God. How much time do you spend on the daily checklist of those who proclaim the Gospel? Do you need more time? If so, how can you get it?
—Daily Bible study
—Daily devotions and prayer
—Daily theological study in the context of
    your tim and place

• Reread the ten commandments of communication. How well do you follow them? Do you break any of them? What could you do that you are not doing now in following these guidelines for communication?
—You shall prepare.
—You shall enter the world outside the church.
—You shall make the connection (between word and world).
—You shall be transparent.

—You shall let your convictions show.
—You shall be practical.
—You shall use your imagination.
—You shall be enthusiastic.
—You shall ask for the order.
—You shall evaluate.

• Videotape one of your messages. Gather two separate focus groups—one of mature Christians and one of seekers. Debrief the message with respect to (1) content (What did they hear?), (2) understandability (What did they understand?), (3) practicality (What do they think they should do with what they heard?), and (4) presentation (Were they engaged by the style?). Compare the results from each focus group. What did you learn? Are any changes suggested that will improve your communication of the good news?

For as I went through the city and looked carefully
at the objects of your worship,
I found among them an altar with the inscription,
"To an unknown god."
What therefore you worship as unknown
this I proclaim to you.

—Acts 17:23

5

Programming for Others

And Jesus came and said to them,
"All authority in heaven and on earth
has been given to me.
Go therefore and make disciples of all nations,
baptizing them in the name of the Father
and of the Son and of the Holy Spirit,
and teaching them to obey everything that
I have commanded you."
                                        —Matthew 28:18-20

The programmatic portfolio of a church for others is neatly summarized in this well-known text from the Gospel of Matthew. The text contains within itself both the "great commission" and the "great commandment"—the call to make disciples and the call to teach them love. This, in a biblical nutshell, is what the church is all about.

Evangelism—inviting people into a reconciled and committed relationship with God in and through Jesus—is the core activity of the Christian church. Not, however, as an end in itself. The great commandment—that we love God and love our neighbor—is embedded within the great commission.[1] Jesus tells his followers that not only are they to invite people into a relationship with him, they are also to teach them "to obey everything that I have commanded you."

What Jesus has commanded us is clear: "I give you a new commandment, that you love one another. Just as I have loved you, you also should love one another. By this everyone will know that you are my disciples, if you have love for one another" (John 13:34-35). The programming of a church for others will actively seek to draw people across the threshold into an encounter with God through Jesus that leads to an intimate relationship with God through Jesus. It will then proactively teach love, not just by talking about love but by creating programmatic opportunities in which love is genuinely experienced, talked about, and encouraged. Salvation does not exist apart from the life of faith—a life of loving regard for God's creation.

We have three basic criteria for developing programs and/or projects at Community Church of Joy:

- Does the program further our missionary vocation to be a church for others?
- Does the program or project meet a real need?
- Does the program or project produce spiritually transformational outcomes?

If the answer to all of these key questions is *not* a convincing yes, a proposed new program or project will not get a green light. If an approved, up and running program or project that initially met these criteria stops meeting them, then the light will go from green to yellow to red.

Furthering our vocation as a church for others

It is very important to take a snapshot of where you are before trying to plan for and implement change. This is particularly true when you are trying to change from being a church for ourselves to being a church for others. If change is going to be successful, the people being asked to change need to see the need for it. They need to be convinced that the change will achieve worthy goals. A statistical snapshot of where you are set alongside an agreed-upon goal of where you want to be can serve to motivate the need for substantial change.

Take a census of every program or project in the congregation by asking three key questions:

- Who is presently participating?
- Who gets invited to participate?
- Who does the planning?

These are simple questions, but the answers to them will be very revealing.

- Who participates in the program or project at the present time? Are all the participants members or old "friends" of the congregation? For example, are all the kids in Sunday school the children of members of the congregation, or is it full of neighborhood kids whose parents may rarely, if ever, go to church? Is church membership a must for joining the softball team, or is it open for anyone in the neighborhood who likes to play ball? Are all the Bible studies for believers only? Do the women's groups include women who may not be members but who are looking for friends, or help with a new baby, or someone to walk with them through a divorce, or advice on parenting, or help dealing with domestic abuse? Ask yourself, who is benefiting right now from the programs of the congregation?

- Who gets invited? When an existing church program is looking for new people, where do you look—in the church directory or around the larger neighborhood beyond the church? Where do you advertise both new and ongoing programs—in the church newsletter or in the local newspaper?

In a church for ourselves, "being one of us" is often the unstated requirement for being welcomed into the various programs and events of the church. In a church for others, however, church membership is not a criterion for participation. Although faith may be the result of participation, faith is not a ticket necessary for admission. Ask yourself, what's the present "price" of admission to the programs and projects of the church?

• Who does the planning? Who are the "gatekeepers" in any particular program? Who are the influencers? Is there a pecking order in the program where those who have been there the longest do the planning? Are there any nonmembers involved in program and project planning? There should be. It is axiomatic that what happens will largely reflect the interests, concerns, and issues of those who do the planning. If the others we seek to serve are not involved in planning the programs and projects that seek to serve them, the chances are high that their interests, issues, and concerns will not be addressed. Ask yourself, who is setting the agenda today?

Honestly answering these questions will give you a pretty good picture of how others are experiencing the ministries of your congregation and will provide some good clues as to what you need to do, and whom you need to work with, in shaping your community of faith into a Jesus community that exists for those who don't already belong to it.

If the picture that emerges is one of programs that curve in on themselves and meet the needs of members only, future programming will need to address the problem. It may be that immovable programs will need to be discontinued and rebuilt from the ground up with a focus on the mission of the church for others. It will be difficult and perhaps painful for some folks to let go of the "for members only" mind-set. A church that has made the decision to become a church for others, however, must stay the course and realign its programming so it serves the mission.

Programs and projects of the church need to be occasions of unlimited grace for those who have been living outside the circle of grace. They should be intentional about inviting and welcoming others. There must be a clear expectation that those on the inside will actively seek to engage those on the outside. In short, the programs and projects of the community of faith have to reflect the missionary consciousness of the community of faith. If they don't, red flags should go up all over the place.

Of course, some programs of the church will primarily meet the spiritual needs of committed Christians, and that's OK to the degree that the program has a missionary consciousness. A Bible study geared for people with a long history of faith would not be appropriate for people with little if any knowledge of either Christian faith or the Christian Scriptures. They need the basics, and it would make no sense to invite them to an intermediate or advanced class. A Bible study for believers would certainly get a green light if the study of the Bible, the reflections on faith, and the applications discussed supported the missionary consciousness of those who participated in it. This would excellently serve the missionary vocation of the church.

This first criterion for developing programs and projects—that it furthers the missionary vocation of the church—is crucial. Without it, the focus on the other becomes *ad hoc,* hit or miss. The common clothesline provides a helpful metaphor for thinking about the church's programs. In many churches, "taking care of ourselves" is the clothesline on which are hung the various programs of the church. If they serve the needs of the membership, there is room for them on the clothesline. Of course, when this is the case, worship for others, ministry for others, and programs for others will find little if any place in the life of the congregation.

In a church for others, however, the clothesline is God's

all-embracing, all-inclusive mission to the world God loves. If you hang the church's programs and projects from *this* clothesline, the focus on the other will be neither *ad hoc* nor hit or miss. That focus will drive everything the community of faith does.

Meeting real needs

"What's the point?" is always a good question to ask when considering a new program or project.

- What will the program do?
- What conditions will the program create?
- Who will do it?
- Whom will it be done for?
- Why go to all the trouble?

If you can't answer these questions in a compelling way, the light should be red. The multiplication of programs that do not serve the missionary calling of the congregation drains precious resources while diverting the community of faith's attention from its primary task—making disciples and teaching them all that Christ has commanded us.

To decide if a need is, in fact, a real need, it makes perfect sense to talk to those who are supposed to have the need. Program planners have to get out of the box of their preconceived notions of what others need and ask them directly what they need. We are back to the importance of taking their order. Focus groups from whatever segment of the community you hope to serve should be an indispensable part of all program planning.

If you are planning a youth program, youth must be an integral part of the planning process. If you arc planning a program for people going through divorce, people who have gone through divorce should be part of the planning process. If you are planning a social ministry to help the homeless, you

need to talk to the homeless on their turf as part of the planning process. If you are planning a worship service for the
folks of Generation Y, a cross-section of that generation has
to have a voice in the planning process. And it goes without
saying that in a church for others, program planners will be
drawn both from those within your community of faith and
from those outside your community of faith.

In inviting the advice of those outside the community of
faith, you must make it clear that there are no strings
attached to the invitation. Don't communicate that you see
them as potential participants in the program. If you do,
your request for advice will feel like manipulation. Make it
clear that you need them as "consultants" in your planning
process. Be up-front about your conviction that the community of faith has both human and divine resources for
personal transformation that leads to fullness of life, lives
rich in meaning, purpose, direction, and joy. Be honest
about your desire for their input in helping you to understand the needs and life experiences of the particular group
you are planning for. Frame it as a matter of wanting to
respect those you seek to serve. Framed in this way, most
of the people you approach will respect your intentions and
be happy to cooperate.

Once a program is up and running, periodic evaluation is
important to make sure:

- you are doing what you said you would do
- the need the program exists to serve is still a real need
  and desired outcomes are being realized
- the program is sufficiently resourced to make a
  difference
- the participant list reflects a healthy mix of mature
  Christians and those who have only recently crossed the
  threshold.

Producing spiritual outcomes

I recommend outcomes-based programming for any church of any size. Programs for the sake of programs is the curse of many a church. When the program is seen as an end in itself, irrelevance, serving the needs of the few rather than the many, bondage to the trappings of outworn traditions, resistance to change, and the squandering of precious resources are all too often the result. When the program is seen as a means to an end, however, the end drives the program and creates a dynamism that seeks to maximize relevance and excellence for the sake of the desired outcomes. Outcomes-based programming is clearly mission-driven programming.

Deciding on appropriate outcomes is, of course, the key to successful programming. Knowing what you want to accomplish and why is the first step. Every program should seek to produce both general and specific outcomes. General outcomes are those that the whole church—including all of its programs and projects—seeks to achieve. By way of illustration, "making disciples" might be a general outcome that drives everything the church does. Specific outcomes are those produced by specific programs. For example, the worship program would not have eliminating hunger as one of its desired outcomes. The soup kitchen ministry, however, would.

Faith, hope, and love—the desired outcomes of a church for others

The first step in programming is the determination of general outcomes, those outcomes that all programs, regardless of their specific goals, will try to produce. At Community Church of Joy, we have decided that all of our programming will seek three general outcomes, all of which are rooted in 1 Corinthians 13:13: "And now faith, hope, and love abide, these three; and the greatest of these is love."

No matter what we do at Joy, we want the result of our efforts to be a growing community of faithful people, hopeful people, loving people who produce faith, hope, and love in the others they serve. These general outcomes stand behind the specific outcomes of every program and project we undertake.

Call her Linda. She was young, a single mom, struggling against impossible odds, feeling unloved and beyond hope. She was one of the others in our midst, loved by God but living outside the circle of grace and faith. She crossed the threshold at Christmastime. She had no food for herself or her children, rags for clothes, no cash, no Christmas gifts for the little ones, nothing. No hope—except perhaps the little spark that brought her across the threshold into our Jesus community.

The community—in the form of one of our social ministry programs—took her in, saw to her immediate needs, and loved her to hopefulness. The specific outcome of the program—caring for needy people in concrete, practical ways—was achieved. The general outcomes that all programs seek to produce were also realized, and in a twofold way.

First, in the person-centered act of caring for Linda, the faith, hope, and love of the program participants was deepened, strengthened, and encouraged. The inner fruits of the Spirit ripened in their conscious effort to follow Jesus into a caring relationship with Linda. Second, over time the experience of being welcomed, accepted, and loved moved Linda from hopelessness to hopefulness, from the margins of faith to the community of faith, and into the fullness of love—the experience of being loved *and* the experience of loving.

The following Christmas, Linda, caught by the vision of God's love for all people, decided to do for others what had been done for her. She became involved in a Joy program that made tens of thousands of dollars available during that special season of Christmas to feed, to clothe, to bring some measure of Christmas cheer to the cheerless, a spark of hope to those who live in a place of no hope.

The material realities of Linda's life had improved and Linda had become a more faithful, a more hopeful, a more loving person. In short, both the desired general and specific outcomes of this social ministry program had been realized.

The nineteenth-century English preacher C. H. Spurgeon said it well: "Faith goes up the stairs that love has made and looks out the windows which hope has opened." That is precisely what programming at a church for others intentionally seeks to accomplish for all who come within any particular program's orbit.

So then, what shall we do?

I find it a good exercise to start with a blank sheet every now and then. Wipe the slate clean. Imagine that you have no programs, no projects, no activities of any kind. All you have is the building(s), the people (in the church and in the surrounding community), and whatever financial resources show up on the income line of your budget. That's it. Keep in mind all that we have said about programming in this chapter and then ask yourself: "As a community of Jesus, as a church for others located in this particular place among these particular people, what should we be doing?" And then let your God-inspired imagination, in the wisdom and power of the Spirit, begin to fill in the blank sheet.

There is no end to the things that can be done and need to be done in carrying out the mission of God. Let your imagination soar. Sitting with other staff, lay leadership, and select folks from the larger community, hold "blue-sky" sessions. Wipe the slate clean and then prayerfully seek to fill it in again with mission-driven programs, projects, and activities.

Such brainstorming releases the creative energies of God's Spirit. Be audacious, bold, daring. Come up with as many ideas, plans, and schemes as you can, caring only if they are focused on bringing faith, hope, and love to God's creation. Don't worry at this stage of the process whether they are doable or not. Don't worry about whether you have the resources, the skills and abilities, the people to make it happen. Use the wondering process. Wonder together, "What would we be like, what would we be doing if we were fully engaged in the tasks of God's mission of love?"

This is a very important stage in the planning process. Brainstorming, blue-skying—call it what you will—*imagining the church as it ought to be is the first step in transforming the church as it is.* Obviously you will need to pare down the list to priorities, goals, objectives, and program plans that (1) are of immediate relevance to your particular context, (2) are doable (with a bit of stretching) in terms of available material, financial, and human resources, and (3) represent a balance between the legitimate needs of members and the needs of the others in the community around you.

Finding balance

Balance is important in more ways than one. Clearly a Jesus community needs to balance its members' needs for care and growth with others' needs. If Christian women and men do not experience and live within the richness of God's blessing in the community of faith, they will be hard-pressed to *be* the richness of God's blessing to, for, and with others. But this is not the only place where balance needs to be sought.

Imagining the church as it ought to be is the first step in transforming the church as it is.

Recognizing that you can't do everything on your blue-sky list forces you to pare it down in a way that seeks programmatic balance with respect to the needs you aim to meet. Single-agenda programming ignores the complexity of human life. Unfortunately, in all too many churches, programming tends to reduce people to caricatures of real women and men. Real people have an amazing constellation of needs—physical, emotional/psychological, and spiritual—that require tending to if wholeness and fullness of life is to be obtained. A church, for example, whose programming essentially revolves around a social ministry agenda may find itself ignoring spiritual or emotional needs. A church whose programming focuses wholly on Bible study and small-group experiences might do fine with the spiritual life and social life of people but miss the boat entirely on issues of physical need or social justice.

A balance of programs, projects, and activities that addresses people in their totality as having a body with its needs, a mind with its needs, and a spirit with its needs is essential in a church for others. No matter how small or how large the church, attention to balance will increase the relevance of your ministry to the world outside the church.

Making it work—or venturing into that beautiful blue sky

You will find it very interesting to compare your blue-sky list of possible programs, projects, and activities with the actual list of things you are currently doing from day to day. I suspect you will discover that the two lists are quite different. We did. We found that what we were doing before we made the decision to become a church for others and what we began to do after we made this commitment were irreconcilable.

We discovered that many of the programs that occupied our time, energy, and resources had long outlived their original purpose. We found that most if not all of our programs were internally focused. They were planned by Christians for Christians which, in and of itself, is not necessarily wrong. As I mentioned before, Christians have legitimate needs and tending to those needs is important. What was wrong with our programming for Christians, however, is that it was done without reference to others. We quite simply failed to focus on the Christian's God-given responsibility actively to love the world outside the church. We did not provide the education, the encouragement, or the opportunity to reach out to the others around us. Our programs did not serve our new sense of missionary calling.

In some cases, you will find that existing programs can be "reinvented." Other-driven outcomes can be added to the program's goals. The program's structure can be opened so that it is inclusive rather than exclusive, welcoming rather than shunning. In other cases, however, you will be faced with the difficult need to shut a program down and redirect the resources, energy, and time of those involved in new directions.

This will anger and possibly alienate people who are quite content with the way things are, and you may need to encourage such people to leave. As the saying goes, "This train is going West. If you want to go East you better get off and find another train." This may sound harsh, but it is necessary. We need to remind ourselves that the church exists to serve God's purposes and not our own preferences. In fact, if we are truly serving God we will probably find ourselves moving again and again outside our comfort zone. God will continually stretch us.

Let's recap the steps for programming in a church for others.

- Decide what are the desired conditions and general outcomes all programs will seek to achieve.

- Take a census of current programs:
   - Who presently participates?
   - Who gets invited to participate?
   - Who does the planning?

- Evaluate current programs by asking:
   - Does the program further our vocation
     as a church for others?
   - Does the program meet a real human need?
   - Does the program produce desired general
     and specific outcomes?

- Decide what programs can be reinvented and what programs need to be shut down.

- Blue-sky/brainstorm with staff, lay leaders, and others about all the possible programs, projects, and activities that could serve your mission as a church for others.

- Compare your blue-sky list with your "reinvented" program list and decide what needs to be added.
  - Look for balance between programs that meet the legitimate needs of Christians and those that meet the needs of others.
  - Look for balance in the kinds of needs that are being met so that the church ministers to whole people.
  - Balance the need for new programs against available resources but make sure you stretch to, and perhaps just beyond, your perceived limits. Trust that God is with you in God's mission.

- Implement, evaluate, fine-tune, carry on, evaluate, improve, and always rejoice in the gifts of God experienced by the people of God as they obediently follow God into mission that matters.

Questions to ponder, things to do

• Take a census of every program presently up and running in your congregation. What does the census tell you about the demographics in your programs? Are they internally or externally focused? What, if any, changes, does the census suggest?

—Who is presently participating?
—Who gets invited to participate?
—Who does the planning?

• Are you presently doing outcomes-based planning? If you are, how is it going? If you are not, why not? What barriers exist to effective outcomes-based planning?

• What are the general outcomes that you would like every program in the church to realize? How should these desired outcomes be communicated to the congregation at large and to those who do program planning? Do you find the "faith, hope, and love" model helpful for outcomes-based planning?

•Evaluate all of your current programs to be sure that:

 — the program has clearly defined objectives
 — you are doing what you said you would do
 — the need the program exists to serve is still a
   real need
 — desired outcomes are being realized
 — the program is sufficiently supported to make
   a difference
 — the participant list reflects a healthy mix of
   mature Christians and those who have only
   recently crossed the threshold.

• Which programs are functioning well with respect to the challenge to be a church for others? Which programs need to be reinvented? Which, if any, need to be dropped? Do you have a plan to make periodic evaluation a standard practice for all programs?

• Try the "blank sheet" exercise (see page 120) both alone and with key leadership. What direction does your brainstorming take you? Are you and your key leadership "reading off the same page" with respect to vision and direction? Where do you go from here?

And whatever you do, in word or deed,
do everything in the name of the Lord Jesus,
giving thanks to God the Father through him.

—Colossians 3:17

6

Money in a Church for Others

Give, and it will be given to you.
A good measure, pressed down,
shaken together, running over,
will be put into your lap;
for the measure you give will be
the measure you get back.

—Luke 6:38

Few pastors like to talk about money. Fewer congregations like to listen to pastors talk about money. And yet it must be done—and without apology. In a money economy, it is the careful stewardship of financial and material resources that fuels ministry. Caring for the hurting, for the hungry or homeless, for the sick or dying, maintaining and expanding church facilities paying utility bills, adding and compensating staff, buying office supplies and educational materials, providing program dollars, and a lot more depend upon the availability of money. Many a church has cut back on staff, delayed necessary maintenance, eliminated programs, and passed up great mission opportunities because the money to support ministry was not there. In a tragically increasing number of small churches the lights go out, the doors are

127

shut, and ministry comes to a full stop because the stream of revenue has dried up.

It should not be that way. Let's be honest. *Dwindling resources for ministry in an age of unparalleled affluence are an indictment of the church*—a sign that the faithful have little faith in the public relevance of the faith. It is a sign that the mission of God has not been truly understood, truly embraced, or truly entered into. It is not, however, an irreversible situation.

Community Church of Joy is a case in point. Twenty-two years ago we were small in every sense of the word: small building, small staff, small numbers in worship, small program, small budget, small vision. Today we are large in every sense of the word: large campus with many buildings, large staff, large numbers in lots of worship services, large program, large budget, huge vision. Although there are many factors in such growth, when a community of faith commits to becoming a church for others, everything changes.

Focus on mission, not money

Congregations that focus on money usually generate more annoyance, resistance, and discontent than money. Congregations that focus on mission generate enthusiasm, commitment, and the resources needed to be faithful in mission. The basics of giving are fairly simple:

- If you ask for my money for things I don't care about, you won't get it.

- If you ask for my money for something I care about, but don't give me a clear sense that giving it will make a real difference in people's lives, chances are I won't give you very much.

- If you ask for my money and I know that giving it will make a major difference, the chances are that you will get more of it.

- If you engage my faith, my understanding, my involvement, and my commitments to God—for mission that makes a difference—and then ask for my money, you will be surprised at my generosity.

All of which is to say that funding the vision in a church for others begins with communicating the vision. Engaging and involving the leadership of the congregation and then the members and friends of the congregation in "wondering" just what the church is all about is the place to start looking for the resources necessary for mission.

Recall our mission statement: *That all may know Jesus Christ and become empowered followers, we share his love with joy, inspired by the Holy Spirit.* This statement emerged from a process—a process of wondering what God wanted for us and from us. It was a public process. That's important. It didn't happen in the quiet of my study or in small closed meetings of a few key influencers. The emerging vision of a church for others was brought to the key leadership in the congregation, and we wondered together publicly if it was of God. Together we refined and expanded the vision, and then we brought it formally to the congregation. More wondering, more conversations, more praying, more arguing, more growth in the corporate understanding of what a church for others was all about and why we should become one. Throughout these conversations, we grew together in the knowledge that our developing sense of what God was calling us to do would require far more resources than we had at the moment.

Our mission statement encapsulates a *spirited* conversation among the people of faith at Community Church of Joy. Without this *prior* conversation, trying to increase giving in support of increased ministry would have failed. We needed to get as many of our people as possible on board with the vision and agreeing that what we wanted to do was what God wanted us to do.

Let's briefly unpack this mission statement, which reflects our public conversation about where God would have us go and what God would have us do. It was our mission statement—and so it will be for you—that set the context for our need for increased resources and provided the framework for effective stewardship. We discovered that our mission statement had to reflect our own relationship with God before we could with integrity move out into the world and invite others into a relationship with God.

- *That all may know.* The fact that God's love extends to all needed to be internalized. Our vital, honest, urgent concern for the well-being of others needed to emerge out of our identification with God's concern for them. Identification with God's abundant love for all people encourages inclusivity on the part of God's people.

- *That all may know Jesus Christ.* It is in knowing Jesus, the one who said, "I am the way and the truth and the life" (John 14:6), that people enter into the presence of God and the fullness of life. In Jesus there is forgiveness, healing and transformation, hope, and reverence for all life. In Jesus, the past—no matter how sordid, no matter how confused or lonely or despairing—is redeemed, caught up into God's future where "death will be no more; mourning and crying and pain will be no more" (Revelation 21:4). Experiencing God in and through Jesus is experiencing life as a gift. When God's people are drawn fully into the heart of Jesus, nothing could be more natural for them than sharing the gift by giving of themselves and their resources.

- *That all may know Jesus Christ and become empowered followers.* Truly knowing Christ is knowing that you stand simultaneously under both grace and the call to discipleship. The individual people of God need to know that their community of faith needs their discipleship if it is to be effective in the mission of God. A Jesus community enables believers to be empowered followers, disciples of Jesus, whose missionary calling is to invite others into the experience of love. The giving of financial resources is a function of discipleship, not a substitute for discipleship. Disciples know that.

- *We share his love with joy.* The public process of crafting a mission statement and educating people into a missionary consciousness lays the foundation for resource development. The foundation is love. As Christian people grow into the wonder of God's nondiscriminatory love, and experience that love in the community of faith, they will begin to hear and answer with compelling clarity and joy the call to a discipleship of love.

- *We share his love with joy, inspired by the Holy Spirit.* In a profound sense, it is here that the rubber hits the road. It is with a note of astonishment that Paul asks the Corinthian Christians, "Do you not know that your body is a temple of the Holy Spirit within you, which you have from God, and that you are not your own?" (1 Corinthians 6:19) The mystery of God's Spirit within us perfecting us in love is a mystery we need consciously to draw the people of God into.[1] Paul's question to the Corinthians needs to be asked with great seriousness to today's Christians: "Do you not know that your body is a temple of the Holy Spirit within you, which you have from God, and that you are not your own?" To ask that question with the people in your community of faith and then to wonder with them what it means that we are not our own is a foundational prerequisite to resource development.

All of which is to say that resource development in support of ministry and mission is rooted in discipleship. Focus on money, and you will barely get by, if you get by at all. Focus on mission, on the transformation of your people into empowered followers of Christ, and the resources necessary for mission will be provided.

Stewardship begins with discipleship. Preaching about stewardship once a year, a month of "money talks" on the need for increasing pledges, and a "commitment Sunday" when people march to the altar and drop their pledges into a plate just won't generate the resources needed for expanding mission in a church for others. Stewardship is a twelve-month, perpetual process, not a one-month special campaign every autumn. In a vital community of Jesus where real needs are being met, where spiritual disciplines that draw people into deeper intimacy with God are taught, encouraged, and expected, and where the fruits of mission are seen in the others who cross the threshold into the community, resources emerge as they are needed.

I imagine some skepticism about my conviction that discipleship leads to stewardship, and I can only respond to it with the words of an old TV advertisement for a popular antacid: "Try it! You'll like it!" Our church did not move over a period of twenty years from a budget well under a hundred thousand dollars per year to one of several million dollars by asking for increased giving once a year. We did it by coming alive to the mission of God and by engaging our people in that mission as empowered followers of Christ.

Let me share with you some of the basic principles that guide our approach to stewardship. They work for us—they will work for you.

Principle 1—All things begin and end in God—even stewardship

It probably shouldn't need to be said, but in a culture where materialistic values make it hard for even Christians to believe in an active, present, responsive God, perhaps it does need to be said. Stewardship is grounded in trust—trust in God. If we trust that God is doing things in the world to draw people into the circle of love and grace, the circle of salvation, and if we trust that God has called the church to do just that, then we should trust that God will provide the resources for the job. If you don't believe any of that, then turn the lights off before you close the door to the church. If you do believe it, then roll up your sleeves, for there is plenty of work to do and God will provide what is needed to do it.

Resource development will only exceed your imagination if you create a climate of expectation. James says it with characteristic bluntness: "You do not have, because you do not ask. You ask and do not receive, because you ask wrongly, in order to spend what you get on your pleasures" (James 4:2–3). The "church for ourselves" asks for itself and shouldn't be surprised when giving falls short and the budget needs to be cut. The "church for others" asks for the sake of mission and shouldn't be surprised when giving exceeds expectations.

I can't say strongly enough how important it is not to focus on money. Focus on mission, focus on what God is doing, focus on the excitement and honor of joining in God's mission, focus on love for the other and *in that context* ask as a community of Jesus for what you need to do the things God is showing you. And believe Jesus when he says: "So I tell you, whatever you ask for in prayer, believe that you have received it, and it will be yours" (Mark 11:24).

In other words, if through the wondering process, through prayer and study, through talking it out as long and as hard and with as many people as possible, you are persuaded that God wants you to move in a certain direction, then get going. Start the work. Take the leap of faith. Commit what resources you have and risk failure. If it is of God it will succeed; if it is not, it won't and shouldn't. I am not talking about irresponsibility. I am talking about doing the hard work of prayerful discernment and then trusting that God is in it and will provide what is necessary. The steps are straightforward:

- Focus on mission—what does God want from us?

- Get people excited. Engage as many people as possible in the wondering process, in prayer and study, in talking about where God might be leading you.

- Pray publicly and confidently for what you need. A quiet prayer with the treasurer or in the privacy of the pastor's study is safe prayer that risks nothing and does not communicate to God's people that in this place God is trusted and we are attempting great things on the strength of that trust.

- Get started. Don't wait until you have all the resources that are going to be needed. We started a multimillion dollar project with only a hundred thousand dollars. As the ministry takes shape and the need for increased resources becomes clear, tie that need directly to what is being done, to the outcomes achieved, and the possibilities for greater outcomes—and then ask. Ask both God and God's people for what you need confidently and with courageous enthusiasm.

Principle 2—The offering begins when the tithe has been given

A church for others, always stretching to reach more people with the gospel, always trying to bring healing and hope to more people, always struggling to care for more people needs a faith community that tithes. Without tithing the mission suffers.

A friend who served as a missionary pastor and professor in Japan for many years told me that the Japanese attitude toward starting new congregations is simple—with only ten people you can do it. If ten people tithe their income, they can provide a salary for their pastor that is the average of the income of the members. The offering, then, goes to pay the bills and provide resources for the programs of the congregation. *The offering begins when the tithe has been given.* We tithe because God asks us to—it is a matter of obedience. The offering that follows the tithe is a matter of thanksgiving. This Japanese attitude is captured in our church's Tithing Plus emphasis.

For most of the last twenty years, Community Church of Joy has followed the traditional pattern of fall stewardship campaigns. Some years were more effective than others; and although we always encouraged tithing during our fall campaigns, it was a hit-or-miss affair. As we grew, added programs and staff, changed locations and turned ourselves more and more into a church for others, we began to realize that if stewardship is a discipline of the Christian life, limiting it to a once-a-year campaign was the wrong way to go about it. As a result, our church leaders made the commitment to develop a process of ongoing, year-round stewardship education that begins at a level appropriate to children and continues through our senior adult programs.

The leadership group committed to leading the congregation toward the goal of becoming a "tithing plus" congregation by the year 2005. Our goal is that by 2005, 51 percent or more of our congregation will be Tithers Plus, folks for whom the offering begins when the tithe has been given. Our church board and staff are leading the way—you cannot ask people to do what their leadership will not do.

Tithing Plus is a strategic process of stewardship education understood as a part of discipleship education. In all of our education programs, in small groups, in worship, in the training of volunteer and professional staff, in new-member integration and in every other activity of the church that seeks growth in discipleship, the relationship between faith and stewardship, between faithfulness in mission and faithfulness in managing wealth, between tithing and the will of God is taught.

Tithing is an ancient tradition rooted in the Deuteronomic law given by God to the people of Israel. In an agricultural economy such as Israel, tithing was tied to the land. The Israelites were to give 10 percent of their grain, wine, and oil, as well as of the firstborn of their herds and flocks. The tithe clearly served to support the priesthood. It was also eaten by the people in festival celebrations of thanksgiving before the God who had given them the land.

The support of the priesthood and the celebration of thanksgiving, however, were by no means the only purpose of the tithe. The gifts of harvest, of wine and oil, and of meat were given to be shared with the foreigners, the widows, and orphans in the land.[2] The tithe served the mission of God by making the blessing of God available to all.

So we teach that the tithe should be the norm for God's people in mission. We need to take God's challenge to God's people—as expressed through the prophet Malachi—with great seriousness: "Bring the full tithe into the storehouse, so that there may be food in my house, and thus put me to the test, says the Lord of hosts; see if I will not open the windows of heaven for you and pour down for you an overflowing blessing" (Malachi 3:10).

We have created an environment in which talking about tithing comes naturally because talking about mission and the needs of mission comes naturally. You can do the same, no matter how big or small you are. We let people know that tithing is the norm, and we encourage them to reach for the norm, but we coerce no one. People will, and should, make their own financial decisions. But we do not apologize for making it clear that for people called by God to the mission of the reign of God, called to bring good news and grace to others, the tithe is normal—normal as an expression of gratitude for grace received and normal as a *minimum commitment* to the world God so dearly loves. Tithing plus. The offering begins when the tithe has been given.

Principle 3—Plan well, and be very public about it

I certainly agree with the old saying that those who fail to plan are those who plan to fail. Good planning is a matter of respect:

- For those you seek to serve
- For those who join you in serving them
- For those who provide the human and material/financial resources that support your service

To ask people to give their volunteer hours and energy and their money to support a program whose goals and objectives are not clearly defined, with no measurable outcomes, no accountabilities, no clear leadership, no plan for raising needed revenues, or accounting for how resources are used, is disrespectful. To put it another way, if you will pardon an expression from the marketplace, every program in the church needs a business plan.

That seems obvious when thinking about a mission center like Community Church of Joy. Along with the tithes and weekly offerings of God's people, we depend on major gifts and grants as well as profit centers to support our growing ministry. A few years ago we felt God leading us to develop a leadership center that would provide much-needed leadership training for Christian leaders regardless of their denominational affiliation. Our goal, of course, was training, equipping, encouraging, and supporting leaders to transform congregations of whatever size into churches for others, centers for God's mission. In keeping with our own mission to the world outside the church, however, our goals for the leadership center we envisioned also include providing character-based, values-driven leadership training for nonprofits, governmental agencies, and the corporate world.

We got to work, held leadership conferences, did some leadership consulting, began preparing leadership resources, and built a solid business plan to take us to the next level. We presented the plan to a Fortune 500 company. They were impressed with the clarity of our vision, the statement of our mission, the value of what we wanted to do, and the detail of our planning—impressed to the point that they gave us a $3 million grant to make it happen. We have followed the same approach in developing a preschool, a kindergarten, and an elementary school, a memorial garden, and a retirement center, all on our 200-acre campus. And there is much more in the offing as we develop programs and facilities to serve the needs of the larger community around us. We do our homework, plan well, move ahead, and trust that God will lead us to revenue sources we hadn't dreamed of.

If you are a leader in a small church, please don't shake your head and put this book down. Let me repeat what I said three paragraphs ago: *Every program in the church needs a business plan*—regardless of the size of the church. Money follows planning because good planning respects those who give.

A business plan for a small church program will tell people:

- What you're going to do

- Why you're going to do it

- Who is going to do it

- How it fits into the overall mission of the congregation
- What resources (human, material, financial) you anticipate needing

- What revenue streams you have (for example, will participants pay a fee or buy the materials they use, will you have a bake sale or church fundraising dinner?)

- What your budget is

- What your desired outcomes are

- What your indicators of success will be

- What the growth potential of the program is.

Once your plan is developed, bring it to the congregation. Get their feedback and their commitment. *And make regular reports to the congregation on how it's going.* To raise the resources needed for mission, you need a congregation that is excited about mission. Enthusiasm for mission is generated when the results of mission are obvious to everyone.

You simply cannot overcommunicate. Tell your people what you plan to do. Tell them what you're doing. Then tell them what you did. And tell them how every dollar committed to the program was spent, making sure that you tie the spending to measurable, observable outcomes. If leadership is transparent and accountable with respect to the way resources are used in carrying out the mission, givers will continue to give and those who have yet to give will now be encouraged to do so. High levels of transparency and accountability let people know that they are respected and trusted, and that in turn earns their trust and generosity.

Principle 4—Create profit centers

The idea of profit centers to support the mission of nonprofit organizations is not a new idea in nonreligious circles, but it has yet to catch on in a big way with churches. Developing profit centers that are compatible and consistent with your mission is essential for building dynamic, growing centers for mission in the twenty-first century. There is simply too much to do. Congregations who are dramatically expanding their reach into the world in ways that are effective and meaningful will demand more resources than they will get in the Sunday offering plate.

We started a separate nonprofit company—the Joy Company—that is developing a retirement village, an aquatics center, a hotel to serve our leadership conference participants, a mortuary and memorial garden, a faith-based book and gift store, a wellness center, and numerous other profit centers. We retain the best attorneys and business minds available to us to help us put all the pieces together. When we need to pay taxes because of unrelated business income, we pay taxes. When we do not have to pay taxes because the income comes from related business revenue, we put the money directly into our mission and ministry.

Again, I urge you not to put this book down if you are a leader in a small church. The scale of your profit centers will be different from those at a church like Community Church of Joy, but the principle is the same. Provide a quality service or product that is compatible with your mission and values and use the revenue to support expanded mission and ministry.

To raise the resources needed for mission, you need a congregation that is excited about mission.

Simple things like retailing organic coffee and homemade muffins on Sunday mornings, having kiosk book sales, renting the church gymnasium (if you have one), to community groups, establishing a fee-based counseling center, holding periodic art and craft fairs, building a small mausoleum on the church grounds for cremated remains, all these are but a sampling of small-scale profit-generating activities that small to medium sized churches can develop to provide additional resources for mission.

There is hardly a church without successful small-business persons or corporate managers sitting in the seats on Sundays.

Use their expertise, harness their skills and enthusiasm by giving them a meaningful roll to play in planning and operating small-scale profit centers. Not only will it generate needed revenues, it is a great way to connect gifted people who spend their days in the marketplace with the mission of God.

Principle 5—Philanthropic support is a key source of resources

America is a tremendously wealthy nation, and our communities are full of affluent people who care about faith and values. Actively seeking their philanthropic dollars in support of the mission of the church is vital to providing adequate resources for expanding that mission. Attracting donors, however, is more difficult than ever before. People with the ability to give are becoming increasingly selective as they have more choices regarding where to spend their charitable dollars. Philanthropic people want to make a difference. They are eager to invest their resources where they see something happening in areas they care deeply about.

Since 1995, close to $10 million has been raised at Community Church of Joy through property and cash charitable gifts. Not only do these gifts enable us to do more of what we are committed to do—reach out to others in every way possible—they are also a sign to us that our ministry matters to philanthropic people because it is meeting real needs.

Do you have a dynamic ministry with kids? Are you doing things that positively shape their bodies, minds, and spirits? Do you want to do more than you can afford to do? Pray long and hard about it. Plan well. Then find out who in your community cares about kids. Introduce yourself to them and them to your program. They are definitely out there. Remember the story I told in the chapter 2 about the woman who bequeathed over $2 million to our church because she cared about kids and had heard about the powerful influence for good we were having in kids' lives through our programs.

Don't be afraid to ask. If you believe in your mission, are

confident that you are doing God's will, and trust that God is changing lives through your faithfulness, then asking for charitable donations is nothing to be timid about.

Principle 6—Provide creative options through planned giving

Development professionals will tell you that the greatest generational transfer of wealth in the history of this planet is taking place right now. As the generation that survived the Great Depression and World War II and then built the amazing economic engine that drove America to unparalleled prosperity in the postwar years dies, the wealth they created is passing into other hands. Planned giving programs provide opportunities for Christians to continue responsible stewardship in support of God's mission after they die.

There are planned giving programs to suit almost any financial situation. I recommend that you consult with a personal financial planner about how to educate your people into ways these planned giving programs can enable them to continue supporting the ministries they care deeply about after they die:

- Charitable Remainder Unitrusts
- Charitable Remainder Annuity Trusts
- Gifts of Property with a Retained Life Interest
- CSOs
- Lead Trusts
- Bargain Sales
- Charitable Gift Annuities
- Life Insurance
- Gifts by Will

The legalese is intimidating and just reading the names of these planned giving options is enough to confuse most of us. A good financial advisor, however, can make it all understandable and help you provide a great service to God's people. Many if not most Christians know little if anything about how planned giving can keep their resources at work in the church's mission long after they have died. Responsible stewardship doesn't end when someone dies, and we do people a service by introducing them to the possibilities of planned giving programs.

Funding the vision means keeping the focus on mission

Generating the resources that a growing church for others needs to be effective in mission is definitely a complex and demanding task, but it is also a rewarding one. There are few opportunities greater than the challenge to fund the vision for experiencing both the faithfulness of God and the faithfulness of God's people.

In the Sermon on the Mount, Jesus gently scolded the "little faith" of those who worried about material things—and money for mission is a material thing! Jesus told his followers to "strive first for the kingdom of God and his righteousness, and all these things will be given to you as well" (Matthew 6:33). If we follow that advice, we will discover to our amazement how prodigal God is through the gifts and service of God's people.

Questions to ponder, things to do

• What is the mission statement of your community of faith? (If you don't have a mission statement, you, together with key leadership, should craft one.) Do your stewardship efforts deliberately implement your mission statement? How can you tie stewardship to the missionary consciousness of your community of faith more effectively?

• What strategies do you have for clearly communicating the vision for mission that calls for increased resources?

• Together with your church council or board, discuss the six principles of effective stewardship (pages 133–43). What changes do they suggest for the way you handle stewardship and the development of resources for mission?

• Who in your congregation or local community can offer you advice and expertise in considering small-scale profit centers to increase revenue streams for mission?

• Who in your congregation or local community can offer you advice and expertise in developing and implementing an effective planned giving program?

• What strategies do you have (or could you develop) for sharing the effectiveness of your ministry with philanthropic people or organizations?

And he said to them,
 "Pay attention to what you hear;
 the measure you give will be the measure you get,
 and still more will be given you".

—Mark 4:24

7

Staffing a Church for Others

We always give thanks to God for all of you
and mention you in our prayers, constantly
remembering before our God and Father
your work of faith and labor of love
and steadfastness of hope
in our Lord Jesus Christ.

—1 Thessalonians 1:2-3

At the heart of mission and ministry are the hearts of those persons who do mission and ministry. The staff of a church for others, be they paid or volunteer, are critical to the faithfulness and effectiveness of a missionary church. Intensive care in the recruiting, selecting, and training of staff is critically important. More than one ministry has floundered over staffing issues.

Years of experience with both small and large staffs of both salaried and volunteer workers has led me to the following observations:

- Failure to match people's natural talents and spiritual gifts with positions that use them well is a major cause of staff burnout and ministry meltdown.

- Failure to think carefully about compatible personality styles, work styles, and leadership styles is a major cause of staff conflict.

- Failure to ensure that a staff person's personal vision and passion for mission aligns well with the congregation's vision and passion for mission is a major cause of conflict within the congregation as a whole.

- Failure to provide ongoing training in both the spiritual disciplines of the Christian life and the ministry-specific skills needed for excellence is a major cause of job dissatisfaction, low morale, and mediocrity in ministry and mission.

Unfortunately, these failures are far too common and the toll in lost energy, lost resources, and lost hope is staggering. Effectiveness in bringing the gospel to the others in our midst demands that we remedy the situation. And it can be done by overcoming the four failures that I have listed above.

Behind these failures usually stands what I call the *warm body model of recruiting*. I can see you smiling as you read those words. I wager there's hardly a Christian leader alive who has not been tempted with *warm body* recruiting. No matter what size the church, there always seems to be more to do than there are people to do it and the temptation to take any warm body who comes along is great. Having a pulse certainly helps, but that is by no means the key qualification for ministry. So let's take a look at strategies for overcoming the four failures noted above, and keep in mind that these strategies are crucial to good staffing decisions whether you are hiring people or signing up volunteers.

Matching people with positions

A good principle to remember is that the person who wants the job is not always the right person for the job. Good staffing decisions are always the result of a process of prayerful discernment. Discernment is a two-way street. The candidate or applicant for a position needs to arrive at an inner conviction that God is calling him or her to this ministry. He or she needs certainty that the ministry is a good match with his or her interests and passions, spiritual gifts, skills, and abilities. The church has to arrive at the conviction that the candidate or applicant for a position is a person called by God to the position. The church needs the certainty that the candidate has the spiritual gifts and moral character, the personal and professional gifts and skills, and the vision and passion for mission that match the position. When the conviction of the church and the conviction of the applicant converge, discernment leads to a positive staffing decision. When they diverge, discernment says it's not a match.

If you are going to match people with positions, you have to know what the position requires. No matter how small or how large the church, it is well worth taking the time to draft detailed position descriptions for *every paid or volunteer position* you have. From church secretary to music director, from custodian to Sunday school teacher, from usher to sound technician, every position should be described on paper with respect to:

- *Relation to mission and ministry*—How is this position important to the mission and ministry of the congregation? In particular, how does this position contribute to the congregation's outreach to others?

- *Tasks to be accomplished*—What exactly needs to be done? How are the components of the position prioritized?

- *Qualifications needed to accomplish those tasks*—Are there any qualifications in terms of prior experience? Are there any educational qualifications? What are the qualifications in terms of knowledge? What are the qualifications in terms of skills? What are the qualifications in terms of spiritual gifts?

- *Amount of time necessary to accomplish those tasks*—How many hours a week are required to do the job? Does it involve evening or weekend commitments? Is the position open-ended, or is it for only a specified period of time?

- *Relationships—Who supervises the position?* Will the position entail supervising others? Where are the points of contact with (1) the other staff, (2) the congregation, (3) the others we are called to serve?

- *Accountability—How will the position be evaluated?* What are the indicators for faithful and effective service?

Taking the time to develop position descriptions that cover these six key areas for every position in the church, be it paid or volunteer, is essential for empowering your various ministries and mission. Knowing what needs to be done and what kind of people you need to do it gives you a tremendous head start.

Writing position descriptions for jobs that are already filled is important for a variety of reasons. On the one hand, going through the process of thinking about the position will either (1) give you the confidence that it does indeed support your mission, or (2) will lead you to the conclusion that it needs to be eliminated because it detracts from your mission. It is crucial to know those things. Particularly in a responsible resource management environment, you shouldn't be wasting precious time, energy, and resources doing things that don't contribute to the mission. On the other hand, writing position descriptions for jobs that are presently filled means that, should vacancies occur, you are ready to move ahead in the search for new people who match the position.

With a position description in hand, applicants for paid positions and candidates for volunteer positions, as well as the leadership of the congregation charged with making staffing decisions, have a benchmark from which to begin the process of discernment. The position description gives both applicant/candidate and church leaders a framework for discerning if there is a match between person and position.

Discernment involves:

- Prayer—searching for the will of God.

- Self-reflection—comparing the person to the position.

- Referencing—thoroughly checking references

- Conversation—talking it through until it's all talked through.

- Decision—Moving to yes or no.

Done carefully and prayerfully, the discernment process will see to it that the right people are doing the right jobs. That alone will release tremendous energy and creativity into your ministries. Discernment-based staffing decisions take their lead from the Apostle Paul:

> For as in one body we have many members, and not all the members have the same function, so we, who are many, are one body in Christ, and individually we are members one of another. We have gifts that differ according to the grace given to us: prophecy, in proportion to faith; ministry, in ministering; the teacher, in teaching; the exhorter, in exhortation; the giver, in generosity; the leader, in diligence; the compassionate, in cheerfulness (Romans 12:4-8).

The value of matching people and their varied gifts with positions is beginning to catch on, and more and more churches are replacing warm-body recruiting tactics with *gifts-based* volunteer recruiting. I can only pray that the practice continues to grow. Let me say it emphatically:

> *Every church, no matter how small or large, should have a person dedicated to helping others discover, develop, and use their spiritual gifts. Every church should make it a priority to nurture people in the understanding and use of their spiritual gifts in all their relationships, be they in the home, the workplace, on the playground, or in the church.*

There are tools available to help you begin a gifts-based recruiting program.[1] In a small church it may need to be the pastor who leads the program, or a volunteer with good people skills and training in gifts assessment. In a medium-sized church, a part-time, salaried spiritual gifts coordinator is a good idea, and in a large church a full-time position for director of spiritual gifts and growth will lay the discipleship base that a church for others is built on.

Balancing personality, work, and leadership styles

The warm-body model of recruiting is ably assisted by the arm-twisting model of recruiting. Together these venerable ways of getting people to do the work of ministry and mission have a high "success" rate in getting people to do things they don't want to do, are not psychologically or spiritually equipped to do, and get no joy out of doing. As a result, the work suffers, people are unhappy and get on each other's nerves, and both paid and volunteer staff become more and more dysfunctional. Paying attention to the personality, work, and leadership styles of the people you recruit and then matching them to both the position *and* the people they will be working with ensures that energy is focused on mission rather than on personal unhappiness and/or conflict with other staff.

In a church for others (in any church, for that matter) people have to love what they do. They should love what they do because they know they are doing it for God.[2] They know they are "not their own," and they know that God has called them to this great work. They should love what they do because it is who they are—it draws out the best in them, their passions, and their gifts. They should love what they do because what they do really matters—lives are changed, people helped, and others are reached with the good news of Jesus. When people love what they do, others not only hear the good news from them, they see the good news in them.

People with a God-given love for little kids will make the nursery a place of outrageous fun and grace for God's little ones. Extroverted personality types will turn your hospitality ministry into an experience of warm and friendly welcome and grace for seekers who

> **When people love what they do, others not only hear the good news from them, they *see* the good news in them.**

risk crossing the threshold into the church. Contemplative personality types will fill the solitary hours of a prayer vigil with power and grace. People who love to work with their hands will keep the grounds and facilities a picture of beauty and grace. People who love the life of the mind will turn teaching opportunities into moments of knowledge and grace. People who like behind-the-scenes detail will count the offering or prepare communion or weed in the garden with both purpose and grace. People who like to interact with others will join action teams and collaborate and cooperate, also experiencing purpose and grace. Folks whose souls soar on the wings of music will turn Sunday mornings into an experience of the divine and grace. People who compassionately weep in the face of suffering will light up a soup kitchen with hope and grace.

I could go on and on. It is a beautiful picture and a possible reality: people loving what they do and doing it with love because it's who they are. Gifts-based recruiting takes people whole, in all their incredible uniqueness and diversity, matches them with opportunities and tasks that answer to who they are, and then sets them loose to serve God and God's people with joy.

Warm-body and arm-twisting models of recruiting need to be deliberately abandoned. The temptation to stay with them, however, is great. It doesn't take much training or work simply to accept anybody who comes along and then arm-twist the congregation to fill the gaps. Gifts-based recruiting, on the other hand, requires building a gifts-based ministry, and that takes extra time and effort. The results, however—ministry flourishes and people flourish—are more than worth it.

As Jean Morris Trumbauer notes, "Our gifts encompass more than our talents. Other aspects of our gifts include our interests, motivations, styles, bodies, values, passions, hopes and dreams, and life journeys."[3] By helping people discern and nourish every dimension of their gifts, we promote spiritual growth and wholeness, and empower their discipleship in the world. Again from Trumbauer: "Gifts discernment must focus on whole people and the entire spectrum of their life contexts—families, friendships, workplaces and schools, neighborhoods and larger communities, and the faith community itself. *Most ministry occurs beyond the congregation*."[4]

This is precisely why a gifts-based ministry and gifts-based recruiting are crucial in a church for others. When the other is the focus of ministry, following Jesus with the best of what and who we are into the world beyond the congregation is just as important as following Jesus within the congregation.

Having a heart for mission

One thing we discovered over twenty years ago is that when we made the decision to become a church for others, not everybody thought that was such a good idea. Metaphorically, most of us wanted to go West, but there were some who still wanted to go East. As leaders, we learned quickly that alignment around common vision and common commitments among both paid and volunteer staff was crucial to moving in the direction we had discerned as God's will for us.

We made total commitment to the congregation's vision for mission an absolute priority in hiring and recruiting volunteers. Having people in leadership positions in the community of faith who are opposed to the common vision encourages the formation of competitive cliques and factions. The result is conflict and chaos. There is simply too much kingdom work to be done to waste emotional and spiritual energy in the kinds of destructive squabbling about what to do and what not to do that has led many a church to do nothing.

In a church for others *having a heart for others* is a non-negotiable requirement for people seeking paid or volunteer positions. Early in the discernment process we seek to discover if the applicant or candidate has such a heart. No matter how excellent the personal and professional skills for ministry, no matter how suited one's temperament, personality style, work and leadership styles are, they cannot compensate for the absence of a heart for others. No community of Jesus serious about its mission to and with others can afford to have staff working at cross-purposes with each other.

I am not advocating for the kind of mindless conformity that sends the message, "My way or the highway." It is simply a question of people being honest about their motives and vision for ministry and then *having the integrity to choose not to work* in a ministry that doesn't match their motives and vision. It's all a part of the discernment process.

Within the context of loyalty to the vision, there are all kinds of possibilities for creativity and innovation. Within the framework of the vision, there is plenty of room for disagreement about how to accomplish the goals and objectives of the mission. In fact, it's healthy. The creative tension that comes from disagreements among people of faith with the same commitments can be the dynamic engine that drives you forward. Conflict can be creative or destructive. It is always destructive when it emerges from fundamentally different visions of what the church should be and do.

A good formula for staffing a church for others might look something like this:

> a heart for others + appropriate gifts =
>
> ministry and mission that matter.

Although both a heart for others and appropriate gifts are essential in the people you seek to fill positions in a church for others, remember that convictions of the heart are difficult to change. Developed, underdeveloped, or undeveloped, if the gift is there it can be nurtured and nourished, strengthened and encouraged, polished up and put to good use in the mission of God. A change of heart is much more difficult to come by.

For that reason, I recommend that if your choices are limited by circumstances and you have to err, then err on the side of heart. At Community Church of Joy, our motto is *always hire for heart and then develop the gifts*. We are never disappointed when a person with a great heart for others and as yet underdeveloped gifts joins us in ministry. Through intentional mentoring and training, gifts begin to glow. We have been disappointed, however, whenever we have hired for gifts and then tried and failed to change the heart.

I won't say it can't be done. The power of God to change a *willing* heart is limitless. And as Paul's experience on the road to Damascus demonstrates, God can even change an unwilling heart. That being said, however, experience shows that the danger of destructive, ministry-debilitating conflict when different hearts for mission collide within the staff of a congregation is too great to take the chance.

Helping people be all that they can be

Once hired, or appointed to a volunteer position, new staffers need to know that they are entering upon the path of perpetual growth. It is an exciting but demanding path and it is only fair to new staff to be clear with them from the beginning that they are *expected* to take advantage of opportunities for spiritual, personal, and professional growth.

Although the dynamics of helping people be all that they can be are a bit different for paid and volunteer staff, the goals are the same:

- The practice of spiritual disciplines
- The development of gifts
- The development of ministry-specific skills

Practicing the spiritual disciplines

Paid staff should expect to be paid for praying and studying the Bible. It's part of the job—no matter what the job—in a church for others. A forty-hour work week for full-time staff is rare in a church doing vital and dynamic ministry, so let's take fifty hours as an average. Now let's tithe. Ten percent of fifty hours is five hours—and that's the minimum amount of paid, on-the-job time a full-time staff person should spend in prayer and Bible study each week. Believe me, it is not unproductive time. If someone is working twenty hours a week as a part-time staff person, the formula is the same: twenty times 10 percent equals two hours of paid time to sit in the office and pray, read the Bible, and have nobody think you are wasting time.

I should be clear that I am not just talking about program staff. From church secretaries to custodians and everywhere in between, all paid staff, whether full or part-time, should know that a minimum of 10 percent of their paid time can go toward prayer and Bible study. This is the natural corollary to believing that God is in the world, that God is leading the church into the world, and that the primary way we speak to and listen to the God who leads us is through the various forms of prayer and Bible study. What could be more important to a Jesus community than a staff that takes God seriously enough to take their own spiritual growth seriously? By giving staff permission to do these things on the job, you send a powerful message: *Our mission is God's mission, and together we will learn from God how to do it.*

At staff meetings, giving half an hour to discuss books like Richard Foster's *Celebration of Discipline* or Dallas Willard's *The Spirit of the Disciplines* is both an opportunity to mentor staff in the development of spiritual disciplines and an opportunity to reinforce the idea that in a church for others you do mission *with* God, not *for* God; and so it is vital to learn how to stay intimately connected *to* God.[5] Toward this end, periodic spiritual retreats are another way to foster both depth and breadth in the spiritual life of your staff.

Volunteer staff also need encouragement to grow spiritually. Providing workshops on the spiritual disciplines for volunteers is analogous to the time spent in staff meetings talking about such things. Those who supervise volunteer staff should continually encourage them in personal prayer, the devotional study of the Scriptures, rest for body, mind, and spirit, and hospitality.

In large churches, you may want to hire a spiritual coach for both paid and volunteer staff. In small churches most of your staff will be volunteers. In such cases the pastor will need to be the spiritual coach, a man or woman of prayer and study who, by his or her example, draws the volunteer staff into the mystery of God in Jesus present and active among us. Nothing will empower ministry more than mentoring staff in the use of spiritual disciplines.

Developing gifts

Implementing a gifts-based ministry is the best way of ensuring that both paid and volunteer staff discover, develop, and use their spiritual gifts. Such a ministry intentionally integrates gifts education into each program in the church. From worship to pastoral care, from new member integration to social justice ministries, from hospitality to youth and family ministries, from faith formation to leadership development, a gifts-based ministry establishes a culture within which it is as natural to function fully in one's gifts as it is to breathe.[6] When people are growing, there is excitement in the air, expectation and hope, enthusiasm. With all that in the air, expect things to happen.

The dynamics of a spiritually alive and growing staff of paid and volunteer workers inevitably spills over into the congregation at large. It's contagious. People want to know what's happening. Why is everyone on the staff so powered up? And eventually they will want to know how they too can begin to experience the same vital, joyful faith that the staff is experiencing.

When seekers cross the threshold into such a church, they too notice that something's in the air, there's something different, and that something promises them the hope and transformation they came looking for. A spiritually alive and growing staff will need to follow Peter's advice: "Always be ready to make your defense to anyone who demands from you an accounting for the hope that is in you" (1 Peter 3:15). In a spiritually hungry world, people of authentic spirituality are like magnets that irresistibly attract those who thirst for God, those who yearn for a transcendent meaning to their lives.

Developing ministry-specific skills

It has often been remarked that most pastors stop reading theology and biblical studies the day the leave the seminary and take up their first ministry. If asked why, the answer is usually that they are just too busy. Well, it's true that all people in ministry—not only pastors—are very busy people. There never seem to be enough hours in the day to do everything that needs doing. Nevertheless, if in the busyness of doing the business of ministry, staff—from the pastor on down—do not take the time to develop the skills and tools of their ministry, sooner or later they will either burn out or dry up. They will lose enthusiasm and satisfaction in their work, and settle for mediocrity in ministry. By neglecting continuous learning in their area of ministry, staff do themselves a disservice, do the community of faith a disservice, and do the others the church exists to serve a disservice.

Successful corporations, be they large or small, spend hundreds of hours a year training their employees. The church for others can do no less. All corporations do continual training to keep a competitive edge, to satisfy customers, to improve production, cut costs, and increase revenues. They are motivated by the bottom line. The community of Jesus is motivated by the bottom line too—we just have a different bottom line. Not profit, but the lives of those God loves and who live outside the circle of that love.

Great corporations also do continual training because they care about the people in the workforce and desire to maximize their job satisfaction, self-esteem, and general well-being. The church for others can do no less. People are the means and the end of the church's mission. Increasing the satisfaction and enthusiasm with which people do their jobs by helping them continually improve their performance and productivity both increases their well-being and increases the quality of their service for and with others.

Again, tithing is a good model to follow. At least ten percent of a staff person's time should be spent in intentional learning, training, and practice. It is a supervisory responsibility to see to it that it happens consistently and well. If five hours of a staff person's week are spent in prayer and Bible study, and five hours are spent in continual training, forty hours of a fifty-hour work week are left for the doing of ministry. They will have forty hours of greater satisfaction and productivity for having given ten hours to intentional spiritual and vocational growth.

It doesn't come naturally. We are all victims of the tyranny of the urgent. In the crunch of accomplishing the endless tasks of ministry the first things to be neglected and set aside are those things that we do for ourselves. Although we may justify this as "self-sacrifice" appropriate to those doing the work of God, we need to remember that the care and feeding of ourselves, tending to our need to stay connected to God and to grow and develop in our vocation, is absolutely essential to accomplishing those endless tasks of ministry.

For both paid and volunteer staff, a budget must be allocated for both continuing education and the purchase of resource materials for growth in ministry-specific skills. So many times I have had both pastors and lay leaders tell me that the money just isn't there for continuing education. The result is that ministry descends into mediocrity, and the budget for the entire ministry goes down with it! The increase in both job satisfaction and productivity that comes from continual training will be more than worth the dollars committed to this purpose. When well-trained, fired-up people do the ministry they love with the excellence that comes from continually improving their skills, ministry ascends to new heights—and so does the budget!

> **Successful corporations, be they large or small, spend hundreds of hours a year training their employees. The church for others can do no less.**

Experienced paid staff should be *assigned* to intentionally mentor new staffers. Building time into busy schedules for the mentoring process is essential. If it is not in the date book, it won't happen. It must be an *expectation* to which people are held accountable in ministry performance reviews. The old adage that if you expect nothing, that's exactly what you will get, is very true. High-expectation congregations produce the results they are looking for. When everyone is *expected to develop their skills continually* and is *expected to help his or her colleagues develop theirs,* the stage is set for continuous improvement. We should never be satisfied with less. Such expectations do not equate with legalism. They equate with the well-being of staff and excellence in mission—the importance of which should be obvious.

For effectiveness in ministry and just feeling good about themselves and what they do, volunteer staff need continual learning as much as paid staff do. *Every program should have a skills training and development component built into it.* Sometimes, senior staff can do the training, such as when the director for youth ministries trains those who volunteer in the program in effective ways of working with teens. Sometimes outside trainers will be necessary, for example, bringing in someone who works professionally in a nursing home or retirement center to train volunteers in ministry to the elderly. Whether your trainers come from inside or outside, structured opportunities for ministry skills training ought to be provided for each program at least once a month. These may be one-hour classes, or half-day workshops, or just half an hour at the beginning of a regularly scheduled volunteer staff meeting. What's important is that it happens regularly so that it has the quality of an expectation. And it must be done with excellence so volunteer staff are truly benefiting by learning practical, applicable skills.

Often the suggestion for regular volunteer staff training in every program of the church is met with the objection that volunteers are busy people and don't want to spend any more time than they have to supporting the ministry. Adding one to three hours of training a month to the time spent actually doing the ministry is thought to be too much. But think of the message you are sending them if you don't regularly train volunteer staff: *What you're doing isn't important enough to do well, and besides that, we really don't care if you do it well and feel good about yourself for having done it well.* In a community of Jesus where we are admonished to see to it that "whatever [you] do, do everything for the glory of God"

(1 Corinthians 10:31), that's not the kind of message we want to send and not the kind of community we are called to be.

In my experience, people who care enough and who feel called enough to volunteer for ministry will not resist the extra commitment of training *as long as it is training that works*. People want practical, useful training that brings results in hands-on ministry and lets them feel good about their contribution. Training that leads to transformation—both of those who are trained and those they serve—benefits everyone.

Together Everyone Accomplishes More —TEAM

It is not without reason that one of the primary metaphors for the church in the New Testament is that of a body. "For just as the body is one and has many members, and all the members of the body, though many, are one body, so it is with Christ" (1 Corinthians 12:12). As the body needs its different parts working harmoniously together according to their particular functions, enabling the whole to accomplish its tasks and desires, so it is with the body of Christ, the community of Jesus. I am convinced that there are no solo successes. No matter how smart or gifted an individual may be, everyone does better and goes further with teamwork. In short, we need each other. We are better together than we are alone. The ability and desire to be a team player should always be one of the principle criteria in making staffing decisions for either paid or volunteer staff.

At Community Church of Joy, we have nine values that we hold ourselves accountable to in building effective teams for ministry:

- People—We believe that all people are created in the image of God and deserve our honor, respect, and understanding, not our judgment and condemnation. Working together as a team is a gift of God and an expression of faith that is active in love.

• Trust—We always seek to behave in ways that earn the trust of others and to act in ways that communicate that we trust them.

• Communication—We always share information, to keep everyone in the loop who needs to be in the loop, and to talk things through until mutual understanding is reached.

• Conflict resolution—We do not avoid conflict but seek its resolution as quickly as possible with direct communication between those involved. We always seek to realize the potential creativity in conflict.

• Cooperation and collaboration—We avoid unhealthy competition and actively seek ways to cooperate for the sake of our mission. We intentionally use our particular gifts to complement the gifts of others for more effective ministry.

• Creativity—We encourage creativity and innovation in each team member and are willing to take risks in experimenting with new ways of doing ministry.

• Sharing responsibilities—We seek an even distribution of work and responsibility among team members so no one is overburdened.

• Rewards—We do not single out anyone for special honors but reward the total team effort and recognize with expressions of gratitude the contribution of all.

- Accountability—We hold ourselves accountable to each other with respect to these values in the spirit of Galatians 6:1: "My friends, if anyone is detected in a transgression, you who have received the Spirit should restore such a one in a spirit of gentleness."

These nine values create the context within which ministry and mission are carried out by God's people at our church. I commend them to you. Keep them before your teams. Encourage your staff to memorize them so they are indelibly etched into their consciousness. Adhering to such values will get you to the next level in staff development.

Paid and volunteer staff are the greatest earthly asset the community of Jesus has in fulfilling its missionary calling. Money, technology, buildings, all of it means nothing without people who share the calling, the faith, and the values of a church for others.

Questions to ponder, things to do

- Describe your discernment process for hiring new paid staff: How do you go about determining if person and position are a match? Who is involved in the process?

- Do you have a formal discernment process for matching volunteers with ministry positions? If so, describe the process and identify who is involved in the process. If not, what would it take to implement such a process in your volunteer recruitment?

- Do you have position descriptions for all paid staff positions? Do you have position descriptions for all volunteer positions? If the answer is no to either of these questions, let me encourage you to draft detailed position descriptions as soon as possible. If the answer is yes to either of these questions, are the descriptions reviewed annually to be sure that the position still meets the need for mission it was designed to serve? Do the position descriptions detail how the position serves the community of faith's mission to others?

• Is your ministry gifts-based? Who in your congregation either has the expertise or could be trained to serve as a spiritual gifts coordinator, helping people to discover, develop, and use their gifts at church, at home, and at work?

• Does the staff have permission to tithe their paid time for prayer and Bible study? If not, what are the barriers to be overcome in establishing such tithing as a normal staff use of time? Does the staff have a spiritual coach to mentor them in the use of the spiritual disciplines? How are volunteer staff mentored and encouraged in the use of those disciplines?

• Does your staff tithe their paid time for continuing education? Do you have a budget to support continuing education opportunities? Is a mentoring system of skill training and development in place for both paid and volunteer staff?

We have gifts that differ according to the grace given to us.
—Romans 12:6

8

Managing Change in a Church for Others

*Pray for us . . . that God will open to us a
door for the word
that we may declare the mystery of Christ. . . .
    Conduct yourself wisely toward outsiders,
making the most of the time.
Let your speech always be gracious,
seasoned with salt,
so that you may know how you are
to answer everyone.*
                                    —Colossians 4:3-6

The somewhat prosaic subtitle of this little book is *Building a Community for Others*. Prosaic perhaps, but instructive. It is worth spending a moment, here at the end of the book, thinking about its three operative words, *building, community, others*, as a prelude to thinking about managing change.

Building takes time

Obviously, a church for ourselves is not going to change into a church for others overnight. Wanting it to be so does-n't make it so. Even in our high-speed, high-tech, instant-gratification world, where we have come to expect a quick fix to all of our problems and a quick realization of all of our dreams, genuine change requires patience, the ability to stay the course, the determination to win through to the end.

The first stage in building is not laying shovel to dirt or hammer to nail. It is planning, and good planning takes time. The second stage in building is not laying shovel to dirt or hammer to nail either. It is gathering the right tools, the right materials, and the right resources needed for the job. That too takes time. If you are too hasty, you may begin with the wrong tools, the wrong materials, and the wrong resources, and your fine building might collapse like a house of cards.

In short, if you want to *Turn Your Church Inside Out,* if you want to build a vibrant church for others and positively man-age the change that it will require, then be patient—prepare well and build strong. The building is in the blueprint; the end of a journey is in its beginning. Good beginnings lead to good endings, although the road may be bumpy and long.

Community is many more than one— or even a few

In seeking to change the church from an organization that exists for itself to an organization that exists for those who aren't members of it, it is good to remember that in the mind of its founder, Jesus, the church is not an aggregate of indi-viduals. Rather it is a community of like-minded folks who care for each other and seek the well-being of all because of their common faith in God's love for all. A community exists because of common commitments, common beliefs, common values, and a common vision of what the *well-being of all* looks like. When commitments, beliefs, values, and vision are not *largely and reasonably* held in common, communities fragment, conflict erupts, and mission gets lost in squabbling.

It is essential to keep in mind at all times that you are building a *community*, and community building has to do with consensus building. It is more than worth the time and effort it takes to bring people along and gain their ownership of the vision. If you only work with those who immediately catch the vision, you will tear down community rather than build it. Again, patience, staying the course, is extremely important.

Finally it's about others, and God's love for them

A great mental shift needs to take place, and it involves a love-motivated leap of faith. In spite of our best intentions, most of us have been well-conditioned to believe the old saying, "Charity begins at home." The whole idea that we should spend ourselves, our time, energy and resources in building a community for people who aren't members of it goes against conventional human wisdom. But that's what God wants, and it is what we must do if we are to be faithful stewards of the mysteries of God.

There is nothing conventional about the gospel. God loves sinners, seeks the outcast, includes the excluded. "You have heard that it was said, 'you shall love your neighbor and hate your enemy.' But I say to you, 'Love your enemies and pray for those who persecute you'" (Matthew 5:43-44). That's not conventional wisdom, but then none of Jesus' wisdom was conventional, as a quick read through the Sermon on the Mount will show.

The good religious folk of Jesus' time thought he was foolish and weak and, according to the ways of the world, his teaching, his life, and his death were indeed all foolishness. The good religious folk of our time, however, would do well to remember that "God's foolishness is wiser than human wisdom, and God's weakness is stronger than human strength" (1 Corinthians 1:25).

Successfully managing the change from being a maintenance congregation to being a center for mission, from being a church for ourselves to being a community for others requires a bedrock, unshakable conviction that *this is what God wants*. Reaching out to others is not an option for the church, it is what the community of Jesus is all about.

Eight principles for managing change in the process of building a community for others

At Community Church of Joy we have learned to embrace rather than escape change. It took us a while to make friends with change, but we did; and we are committed to an ongoing courtship with change. Along the way we have learned some important principles for welcoming and managing change in such a way that the changes necessary for faithfulness and effectiveness in mission are fully integrated into the whole life of the community. Nonintegrated change is like trying to hold an airplane's wing on with a band-aid. It isn't going to fly. More than one pastor (and congregation) has crashed and burned because attempted changes were not worked into the fabric of congregational identity and life.

After over twenty years of learning—often the hard way—from experience, we have reduced the dynamics of change management to eight easily grasped principles. Following them will not guarantee that change is painless, but it will help to ensure that change integrates well into the life and practice of the whole community and serves the mission.

Change begins with leadership— leadership begins with the pastor

In our democratic, egalitarian society, Americans are often suspicious of authority, of anything that smacks of a hierarchical ordering of things. From the eighteenth-century Boston Tea Party to the *Question Authority* bumper stickers of the sixties to the postmodern relativism of the new millennium, Americans have a demonstrated history of not wanting to be told what to do. This can be good—our political and social freedoms are grounded in this egalitarian strain in the American psyche. It can also be bad. When authority is radically questioned and resisted, it is impossible for communities to move ahead.

American churches tend to be democratic organizations with their leaders acting like elected officials, that is, serving at the will of the people. The problem, however, is that the church is not solely reducible to a democratic organization. It is the "body of Christ," a body of which "Christ is the head." At a profound level, the leadership of a church—elected or not—does not serve at the will of the people, *it serves at the will of God.*

The office of pastor is established by God to serve God's purposes. "The gifts he [God] gave were that some would be apostles, some prophets, some evangelists, *some pastors and teachers, to equip the saints for the work of ministry,* for building up the body of Christ, until all of us come to the unity of the faith and of the knowledge of the Son of God, to maturity, to the measure of the full stature of Christ" (Ephesians 4:11-13).

To be a pastor and teacher in the body of Christ is an awesome responsibility and high privilege. The pastor is called by the congregation to this responsibility and privilege by virtue of his or her biblical education, theological training, and rootedness in the traditions of the faith. It is this grounding that protects the faithful from demagoguery.

Part of the pastor's responsibility and privilege is to "wrestle with God" until he or she receive God's vision for mission for the community of faith. This wrestling takes long hours of prayer, Bible study, and learning the realities, the makeup and needs, of one's particular social/cultural location. It may take long hours of listening to the "others" in the larger community as well as listening to the members and friends of one's community of faith.

Personally knowing the vision, having confidence in your understanding of what God has called you and the community of Jesus to do at this time in this place, is the crucial first step in moving from vision to reality. Such confidence comes from doing the hard work mentioned in the previous paragraph. A pastor who has not wrestled with God in these ways to the point of confidence in the vision will not be able to provide the leadership needed to guide the process of change creatively. The pastor who has wrestled with God in these ways will be able to speak with authority and not as an authoritarian—a vital difference.

Change continues with leadership— enlisting key leaders is the key

Once the pastor has prayed, studied, and talked his or her way through to a valid, vibrant vision for mission, the wisdom and support of key leaders in the congregation must be sought. The importance of having men and women in key leadership positions who themselves are faithful in prayer and study, and who model for the congregation lives of discipleship, cannot be overstated. Warm-body recruiting for the folks who sit on the church council or board should never happen—even if seats need to be temporarily left unfilled.[1]

In both formal and informal settings, the pastor needs to lay his or her vision for mission before the church board with the conviction that God has disclosed to him or her the vision and the conviction that, through public discussion of the vision, God will continue to refine it. None of us is wise enough alone to comprehend fully the length and breadth, the height and depth of God's will for the church and the world. If a pastor has the confidence that the way ahead has been disclosed, and the humility to see that the collective wisdom of the community's leaders will help to straighten the way, he or she will be in a position to fine-tune the vision and gain the necessary level of ownership on the part of the board.

This may be a lengthy process, and agreeing up front on how long it should take will help to ensure that the process doesn't get bogged down in meetings and conversations that finally don't go anywhere. In my experience, three to six months is adequate. Agreeing as a board that the visioning process will be completed within a fixed period of time will help to keep the process focused. Consideration of the vision should be done in a "committee of the whole" with the pastor—not the president or chair of the board—moderating the discussion. The final vote to adopt the vision should follow the normal procedures of the board.

It is vital in managing change that the vision be related to all programmatic areas of ministry. If we adopt this vision, what will our worship look like? If we adopt this vision, what will our educational programs look like? If we adopt this vision, what will the impact be on our youth programs, programs for singles, programs for the elderly, social ministry programs, and hospitality program? Staff, key leaders and board members with responsibility for these areas of ministry need to report to the entire leadership team their understanding of how the vision will affect their ministries.

To manage change successfully, the impact of the change on *every aspect of the organization* has to be considered, understood, and accepted by the organization's key leadership. The pastor, senior staff, and key leadership have the ongoing responsibility of casting the vision before the whole community of faith and need to understand and be able to interpret what the vision means for the whole community.

Once senior leadership has helped to fine-tune the vision, and then has committed to the vision, the next tier of leadership should be brought on board. These will be those who provide ground-level leadership in each program. The worship committee or team, Sunday school teachers, hospitality organizers, social ministry coordinators, youth leadership—all should be convened as individual ministry teams in workshops where the (1) the vision is cast with enthusiasm, (2) the impact on the ministry is presented with enthusiasm, and (3) feedback is solicited with enthusiasm.

At this level, leadership is not asked to specifically adopt the vision—that has already been done by the staff and the board—but they are asked to commit to it. The message should be clear: this train is going West and here's what the journey will be like. Feedback should be *honestly* solicited, not as a tactic to make people feel good, but as a means to fine-tune the vision further *at its operational level.* Those who actually do the hands-on ministry will have good ideas about how to implement the vision. Listening to them and letting what you hear help to shape the operational implementation of the vision is both a practical approach to planning and a proven way to gain ownership of the vision from on-the-ground leaders. Without such ownership, the vision will falter.

The response of ground-level leadership will be mixed. Some will embrace the vision and its necessary changes with great enthusiasm right from the start. Some will be reserved with a wait-and-see attitude—not actually resisting but needing to be convinced. Some will resist the whole thing, both the vision and necessary programmatic changes. That's OK. In fact, it's probably healthy—to a degree. Those who immediately embrace the vision will help create the momentum needed to integrate the change into the life of the community. Those with a wait-and-see attitude will be an encouragement to senior leadership to cast and recast the vision with ever-increasing clarity and comprehensiveness. Those who resist will be a foil against which the vision is sharpened—and they just might have good reasons for their resistance, which senior leadership needs to hear. The challenges of those who resist should never be dismissed out of hand. They should be listened to. It just may be that those who resist change are speaking prophetically.

The time may come, however, when senior leadership will have to tell those who continue over time to resist the vision actively that their participation in the program is no longer possible. If they cannot support the common vision of the congregation, personal integrity requires that they withdraw and not continue to subvert the will of the community with their resistance. It is difficult to ask people to withdraw, but successful change management requires that leadership share a common commitment to and passion for the vision. Within that commitment there is plenty of room to disagree about the particulars of how to implement the vision, but if common commitment and passion are not there, the chances are great that the change will be derailed.

The commitments of the leaders are a model for the whole community

You will find it difficult, if not impossible, to integrate and manage change if the change is not reflected in the personal commitments and behavior of key leadership. Leaders lead. It is as simple as that. As part of the visioning process with the leaders, the implications of needed changes for the way leadership conducts itself need to be forthrightly discussed.

At our church we have certain expectations of leaders that go hand in hand with leadership in a church for others.

- We expect leaders to worship regularly and to model hospitality to seekers who cross the threshold on Saturday evenings and Sunday mornings.

- We expect leaders to be men and women of regular prayer and Bible study.

- We expect leaders to practice tithing.

- We expect leaders to participate in service or mission projects that directly fulfill our common commitment to be a church for others.

- We expect leaders to engage in perpetual learning.

- We expect leaders to support creative, innovative, risk-taking initiatives in mission and ministry.

It is a matter of respect and integrity that you should not expect people to do anything that their leaders will not do. If leaders will not go the extra mile for mission, it is unlikely that those they lead will either.

Let me repeat a point I made earlier. A high-expectation church is not a legalistic church. We coerce, judge, or shame no one. We do, however, set standards for leadership and expect leaders to accept the challenge for the sake of mission. If, for whatever reason, someone feels that he or she cannot make the commitments expected of leadership, their decision is respected. They are asked, again as a matter of integrity and respect, not to seek or, as the case may be, to withdraw from, leadership positions.

Communicate what's going on to everyone

People are much more likely to resist—and sabotage—change when they don't know or understand what's going on, and why it is going on. As Lyle Schaller once told me, people are usually down on what they are not up on.[2] Remember the story of George that I told in the first chapter. Without knowing or understanding the changes we were proposing, George informed me that he was going to cast dissenting votes on everything we were planning.

Change is normally resisted because of fear. The Bible tells us rightly that perfect love casts out fear. Knowledge and understanding, however, also help. Once both senior and ground-level leadership is onboard with the vision, the members and friends of the church have to be brought onboard. You need to get everybody talking about the change *publicly*. Nothing will sabotage change more quickly than private, "behind the back" criticism of change. This potential bomb can be quickly defused by giving people plenty of public venues for talking through the issues and coming to grips with the implications of change.

Public discussion is the best way to handle criticism. If it is negative, carping, destructive, wet-blanket criticism, its public display will show it up for what it is. If it is creative, constructive criticism, public expression of it, and its respectful hearing by leadership, will go a long way toward bringing the critics on board.

In communicating the vision and its necessary changes to the community of faith, a coordinated approach is necessary. Focus groups, town meetings, special messages during worship, newsletters, special mailings, adult forums, guided Bible studies, small group discussions—these are all venues for casting the vision and educating people about what it means for them, for the church, and for the others the church seeks to serve.

If necessary, invite people to leave

This is never easy, but many foundational changes have failed because people who militantly refuse to accept the change and actively resist it were not asked to leave. People can become very proprietary about the church. Many times I have been told by folks, "You can't do this to *my church!*" At such times people need to be reminded that it is God's church and that we are trying to discern God's will for us.

Naturally, if one or two people are trying to speak for God in the face of the whole congregation, serious questions should be raised about their vision. If, however, you have followed the trajectory of discernment that I have outlined here

pastor → key leadership → ground-level leadership→
members and friends

and let each level contribute to the fine-tuning of the overall vision and direction, it will not be the case that only one or two people are speaking for God. The community of faith will be responding to the movement of God among them.

People who seek to derail change should not be allowed to subvert the community of faith in its move to become a church for others. You may choose to go the extra mile with them, but don't invite them for the whole journey if they demonstrate over and over again that they want to go in a different direction. For the sake of the community, and for their sake, they need to be asked to leave.

Work the change into each and every program

The move from being a church for ourselves to becoming a church for others will, in one way or another, affect every aspect of the community's life together. It has to be carefully thought through. If the change is not consciously worked into all programs and projects, the integrity of the change will be threatened. If certain programs or projects are left out, consistency will be lost and the church will fragment into old and new ways of doing things.

People will want to know what the new vision for ministry and mission for others will mean for the programs, projects, and activities that they care about and are involved in. It is imperative that leaders know exactly what that impact will be and are ready to explain it clearly and enthusiastically. The watchword for leaders is:

> *Take every opportunity to cast the vision,*
> *and make it concrete and practical!*

When explaining the impact of major changes on specific programs, change needs to be justified in terms of desired outcomes. People will want to know what is at stake. What will be gained if the change is successfully implemented? What will be lost if the change fails?

If every program, project, and activity is drawn into the change from the ground up, as it were, tremendous momentum for change is generated. People are energized by change when it is purpose-driven, and all-inclusive. Add to this the conviction that this change comes from the heart of Jesus in his unconditional love for others, and the energies of unlimited grace will operate at the core of your change management.

Provide continual updates

Although it's very important, getting people to go with change is only the first step in successfully managing change. The second step is maintaining momentum as you implement the change. The third step is to evaluate the impact of the change on your ministries and mission. The fourth step is to either do midcourse adjustments or initiate new changes as the context and circumstances of ministry and mission dictate.

To navigate these stages of change management successfully, you must keep people informed of what's going on and what it means. Too many organizations romance failure when they close down channels of communication after successfully negotiating step one.

As you implement change, be sure to provide continual, compelling updates to the members and friends of the congregation. Let them know what's actually happening as a result of the change. What outcomes are actually being realized? What surprises have you encountered? What still remains to be done? What failures have you experienced? What have you learned in the implementation process? Do you need anything from them? What should they be praying about?

People will stay engaged if they are invited to stay engaged and are given enough information (1) to know what is going on, (2) to have their questions answered, (3) to give meaningful feedback, and (4) to feel a vital part of the process. An informed and involved community of faith is essential to effective change.

Provide complete budget information

This final principle for effective change management is one that is almost always overlooked. It shouldn't be. If you are asking people to fund the vision, to underwrite the changes that will turn them into a church for others, they deserve an accounting.

Regular budget reports that show clearly how resources are being allocated to support the change in every program and project, in staffing, in training, and in facilities management create a climate of trust—which is absolutely essential to the healthy and successful implementation of change. Be careful to show not only how money is allocated, but how it is actually spent. Again, tie spending to objectives and outcomes. What is being accomplished, what mission objectives realized as a result of the spending? Are there any budgeting errors? Be honest about them. Do you need to shift money around from one budget line to another? Explain the reasons in terms of mission effectiveness. Have unanticipated funding needs arisen? Share them and ask for a response.

Financial transparency is the eighth factor in successful change management which, taken together with the other seven principles for managing change, will create a climate within which change is embraced rather than rejected. The mission of God to the world God loves is more than worth the care and effort to manage change well.

Questions to ponder, things to do

• What is your community of faith's current attitude toward change? Do they tend to embrace change or resist change? What accounts for their attitude?

• With respect to visioning, does your community of faith follow the "trajectory of discernment"—pastor → key leadership → ground-level leadership → members and friends? If you do, has it given you the critical mass necessary to move ahead? If you don't, what stands in your way to giving it a try?

• If you are the pastor, have you wrestled with God long and hard enough to discern a vision for mission? If you have, have you formulated it into a comprehensive plan for ministry and mission? If you haven't, what prevents you from wrestling with God? What can you do about it?

• Gather your key leadership and discuss the eight principles for managing change within the framework of your community of faith. Be concrete. What will each of these principles mean in your circumstances? Can you agree to follow them?

For surely I know the plans I have for you,
says the Lord,
plans for your welfare and not for harm,
to give you a future with hope.

—Jeremiah 29:11

Afterword

This book is an invitation to join in the journey that is reflected in its pages. The vision that has driven me for all of my adult years—a vision of the church of Jesus Christ reshaped, transformed into a Jesus community for others—still moves me to work with pastors and Christian leaders of all denominations in making the vision reality.

If you have found ideas in this book that move you to share this vision, then I encourage you to do two things. First, share the book with your key leadership. Spend one evening a week for eight weeks discussing each of the eight chapters. Answer the questions at the end of each chapter and then go to the next level and talk through whatever issues, concerns, and ideas emerge from answering the questions. And then plot your own journey to transformation.

Second, as you embark on the journey of transformation into becoming a Jesus community for others, invite us at Community Church of Joy to travel with you. Visit our web site at www.joyonline.org. There you will find resources to help you on the way. You will also find a dedicated e-mail link that will (1) allow you to get further help with ideas in this book, (2) answer questions you may have about the book, (3) get a response to any challenges or concerns you may have with what you have read here, and (4) give you an opportunity to share with us and others on the journey your own experiences, insights, and advice on becoming a community for others. We are also offering a web-based discussion forum around the book and the idea of transforming congregations into communities for others. Here you will be able both to post and respond to messages as well as interact and network with others online who share your commitments to mission. Should you decide to use this book as a foundational resource in transforming your church, we would be happy to establish an email consultancy with you and would be glad to consider arranging an onsite visit by some of our Leadership Center staff to help in your planning and implementation.

This book, of course, is a big-picture effort. It is designed to make the case for transforming churches into communities for others, to motivate Christian leaders to commit to the vision, and to lay the foundation for such a transformation with practical advice for getting started. Much more can and needs to be said about all of the topics covered in *Turn Your Church Inside Out.* I am planning several in-depth, workbook-style resources on these and other topics to give Christian leaders a tool kit for transformation as we move into the third millennium.

May our God of love beyond reason and of uncontainable joy give you the amazing grace and awesome power to turn your church inside out.

Notes

Chapter 1

1. Dietrich Bonhoeffer, *Letters and Papers from Prison* (London: SCM Press, 1971) 382.

2. Rudy Wiebe, *The Blue Mountains of China* (Toronto: McClelland and Stewart, 1970) 215–16.

3. Todd Hahn, "A Postmodern World," *Joy Leadership Center,* #1, October 1999, 1.

Chapter 2

1. Walter Rauschenbusch, *A Theology of the Social Gospel* (Nashville: Abingdon, 1981) 102.

2. Michael Foss, *Power Surge: Six Marks of Discipleship for a Changing Church* (Minneapolis: Fortress Press, 2000) 91.

3. For more information on evaluating ministries, see Walther Kallestad and Steven Schey, *Total Quality Ministry* (Minneapolis: Augsburg Books, 1994).

Chapter 3

1. Charles Trueheart, "The Next Church," *Atlantic Monthly,* August 1996), 37.

2. Max Lucado, quoted in *The Inspirational Bible* (Nashville: Word Publishing, 1995), 694–95.

Chapter 4

1. This text summarizes one of the Bible's best encapsulations of the gospel, 1 John 4:7-16.

2. Michael Foss, *Power Surge: Six Marks of Discipleship for a Changing Church* (Minneapolis: Fortress Press, 2000) 89.

3. Cf. 1 Corinthians 1:17–2:2.

4. Quoted in Leonard Sweet, presentation at Joy Leadership Center, October 1999.

5. Quoted in Tim Kimmel, *Basic Training* (Nashville: Thomas Nelson, 1997), 72.

6. See *The American Heritage Dictionary of the English Language, Third Edition* (Boston: Houghton Mifflin Co., 1992).

7. From a personal conversation.

Chapter 5

1. "One of them, a lawyer, asked him a question to test him. 'Teacher, which commandment in the law is the greatest?' He said to him, '"You shall love the Lord your God with all your heart, and with all your soul, and with all your mind." This is the greatest and first commandment. And a second is like it: "You shall love your neighbor as yourself." On these two commandments hang all the law and the prophets.'" (Matthew 22:35-40).

Chapter 6

1. Cf. 1 John 4:12-13: "No one has ever seen God; if we love one another, God lives in us, and *his love is perfected in us*. By this we know that we abide in him and he in us, because *he has given us of his Spirit*.

2. Cf. Numbers 18:21; Deuteronomy 12:17-18; 14:28-29.

Chapter 7

1. Three resources to help you begin a gifts-based volunteer recruiting program are: Jean Morris Trumbauer, *Created and Called: Discovering our Gifts for Abundant Living* (Minneapolis: Augsburg Fortress Publishers, 1998); Lloyd Edwards, *Discerning your Spiritual Gifts* (Boston: Cowley Publications, 1988); Bruce Bugbee, Don Cousins, and Bill Hybels, *Network: The Right People in the Right Places for the Right Reasons* (Grand Rapids: Zondervan, 1996).

2. Cf. Romans 14:8; 1 Corinthians 10:31; Colossians 3:17.

3. Jean Morris Trumbauer, *Created and Called: Discovering our Gifts for Abundant Living* (Minneapolis: Augsburg Fortress Publishers, 1998) 21.

4. Ibid., italics added.

5. Richard Foster, *Celebration of Discipline* (San Francisco: HarperSanFrancisco, 1988); Willard Dallas, *The Spirit of the Disciplines* (San Francisco: HarperSanFrancisco, 1991).

6. See Trumbauer, *Created and Called* 27, for a diagrammatic look at how gifts education can permeate every ministry in the congregation.

Chapter 8

1. Different congregations have different names for their chief governing body, *church council* or *church board* being the two most widely used. For narrative simplicity, I will use the term *board* in what follows and ask the reader to substitute whatever the governing body in his or her church is called.

2. From a personal conversation with the author.